Collaborative Working

Alan Lawrie and Jan Mellor

DIRECTORY OF SOCIAL CHANGE

'This practical guide will be of real benefit to trustees and managers considering working more closely with others to achieve their objectives. The step-by-step approaches will ensure that the difficult questions are asked while the gentle reminders around charity law, TUPE and other legal matters are there but in their correct place, i.e. not as the overriding issues. The case studies provide positive messages while highlighting some of the pitfalls and will be of assistance to the reader. This book can never give all of the answers to collaborative working at any level but will take away much of the mystery, helping the reader understand better this complex but current issue.

'Charities are always under pressure to merge, often from those who see merger as the solution to commercial inefficiency without understanding the different drivers. This book will help those in charities understand the steps they can take, short of a full merger, to achieve efficiency in service delivery and beneficiary support through many different types of collaboration. Get it on the bookshelf and use it when you need it!'

Nigel Scott, Course Director,
London South Bank University

'Whether a veteran seeking to improve practice, or relatively new to collaborative working, this concise, comprehensive toolkit and guide has something to offer both practitioner and decision maker on the subject. I found it invaluable for challenging organisational motivations and received wisdom, as well as exploring risks, hazards and potential outcomes of the complex landscape of collaborative practice including full organisational mergers. It provides organisations with a route map to navigate the potential pitfalls and reap the benefits of joint working, ensuring they understand how to tailor good practice to their own evolving needs. I can't recommend it enough.'

Lainya Offside-Keivani, Chief Executive,
Abbey Community Association, Westminster

'When is a book really useful? When it comes along when you really need it. I like this book particularly because, as Acting Chair of a youth project locally, I am faced with the withdrawal of County Council funding at the end of March as they 'reconfigure' (or cut as we call it).

'I already had been looking at the merits of working with others so the fact that this book contains not only many examples of working together practices (alliances, joint bidding, shared services, consortia, mergers and so on) but also exercises designed to help settle upon answers which meet one's needs, makes it invaluable.

'This is a thorough and well-argued book designed to help thinking processes – there is a lot of detail, there are case studies (including the option 'not to' at the end of the day) and there are no pat answers. *Collaborative Working* is a valuable and helpful contribution at a time when all of us need to be thinking about how we best serve those for whom our organisations exist rather than serving our organisations for their own sakes.'

Jan Cosgrove, National Secretary,
Fair Play for Children

Published by the Directory of Social Change (Registered Charity no. 800517 in England and Wales)
Head office: 24 Stephenson Way, London NW1 2DP
Northern office: Federation House, Hope Street, Liverpool L1 9BW
Tel: 08450 77 77 07

Visit www.dsc.org.uk to find out more about our books, subscription funding websites and training events. You can also sign up for e-newsletters so that you're always the first to hear about what's new.

The publisher welcomes suggestions and comments that will help to inform and improve future versions of this and all of our titles. Please give us your feedback by emailing publications@dsc.org.uk.

ISBN 978 1 906294 69 4

British Library Cataloguing in Publication Data
A catalogue record for this book is available from the British Library

Cover and text design by Kate Bass
Typeset by Marlinzo Services, Frome
Printed and bound by Page Bros, Norwich

MIX
Paper from responsible sources
FSC
www.fsc.org   FSC® C023114

Contents

 Chapter two

The collaborative working process 17

Chapter three

Alliances 43

Chapter four

Joint working 51

Chapter five

Lead partner and subcontracting models 61

Chapter six

Consortia and joint ventures 77

Chapter seven

Group structures 89

Chapter eight

Mergers 95

Chapter nine

Making collaborative initiatives work 127

References 139

Further reading 140

Index 141

About the authors

Jan Mellor is a knowledgeable and enthusiastic advocate of the not-for-profit sector and is passionate in her belief that good management is what makes the difference between organisations that deliver and those that don't.

Jan now works for a national charity and has worked in the not-for-profit sector in many capacities: as a project worker for a young people's project, the Director of a medium-sized national voluntary organisation, and a management trainer and consultant. Her main interests are in governance, organisational change and management development.

She is co-author of *The Complete Guide to Surviving Contracts* (2008).

Alan Lawrie has worked as a full-time independent consultant for 20 years and specialises in strategy, business planning, and commissioning and organisational development.

Before moving into consultancy Alan worked as a development worker, trainer and manager in the voluntary sector and then moved into management roles in the public sector.

He is the author of *Managing Quality of Service* (1984 and 1995), *Developing Your Organisation* (2000), *The Complete Guide to Business and Strategic Planning* (1988, 1994 and 2007), *Managing Contracts: A Resources Pack* (1988 and 1994), *The Complete Guide to Creating and Managing New Projects* (1999, 2002 and 2010) and co-author of *The Complete Guide to Surviving Contracts* (2008).

Jan and Alan have helped several organisations to explore ways of collaborating and worked with them to develop successful formats for collaboration.

About the Directory of Social Change

The Directory of Social Change (DSC) has a vision of an independent voluntary sector at the heart of social change. The activities of independent charities, voluntary organisations and community groups are fundamental to achieve social change. We exist to help these organisations and the people who support them to achieve their goals.

We do this by:

- providing practical tools that organisations and activists need, including online and printed publications, training courses, and conferences on a huge range of topics;
- acting as a 'concerned citizen' in public policy debates, often on behalf of smaller charities, voluntary organisations and community groups;
- leading campaigns and stimulating debate on key policy issues that affect those groups;
- carrying out research and providing information to influence policymakers.

DSC is the leading provider of information and training for the voluntary sector and publishes an extensive range of guides and handbooks covering subjects such as fundraising, management, communication, finance and law. We have a range of subscription-based websites containing a wealth of information on funding from trusts, companies and government sources. We run more than 300 training courses each year, including bespoke in-house training provided at the client's location. DSC conferences, many of which run on an annual basis, include the Charity Management Conference, the Charity Accountants' Conference and the Charity Law Conference. DSC's major annual event is Charityfair, which provides low-cost training on a wide variety of subjects.

For details of all our activities, and to order publications and book courses, go to www.dsc.org.uk, call 08450 777707 or email publications@dsc.org.uk.

Foreword

This is a welcome and timely book. Welcome because it hands the reader a route map to negotiate the complicated junctions and unlit avenues of collaboration. Timely because it I know of no organisation at this time that isn't currently exploring one form of collaboration or another.

But is it any good? I am relieved, as the writer of the foreword, to be able to say that the book is better than good. It is an excellent resource that anyone in the voluntary sector would find useful – from the big national charity CEO right through to the secretary of a neighbourhood group. What the writers Alan Lawrie and Jan Mellor have done for all of us here is to provide a proper intellectual framework for exploring collaboration in its various forms. This is a first and we owe them thanks.

But their biggest achievement has not simply been to explain the various approaches to collaboration. It has been to give us the practical tools we need to take our own organisations' thinking to the next level. What you're getting here, as part and parcel of the book, is a set of superb guides for topics that can be used in workshops and self-checklists on what you need to be thinking about at any given stage on your collaboration journey.

So what is the book really saying? The core message here is that collaboration isn't just about mergers or takeovers. It can also be about a range of other things: consortia, joint ventures, alliances, group structure, informal alliances, sub-contracting and partnerships.

When I had finished the book I thought a lot about what it meant for me. My conclusion was that it underlined the important of three things: people, process and purpose. Collaboration is, first and foremost, about people and dissolves when people can't trust each other or see their interests to be in conflict. Secondly, for collaboration to work, you need a strong process – like scaffolding round a building while the work takes place. Thirdly, and most importantly, you need purpose. The most powerful collaborations featured in the book occur when the outcomes captivate and galvanize everyone involved. Where one plus one equals 64, it has to be worth it.

What really sets this particular book apart is its ability to help the reader work out which collaboration tool is right for them. Like many of you, I am a grizzled veteran of the voluntary sector scene. I have led a big merger. I have also been both midwife and executioner of a number of consortia and partnerships. I hold no illusions.

But what I like about Alan and Jan's work is that they don't either. This isn't in any way airy-fairy or idealistic about collaboration. Reality shines through from the authors and in the voices of real people who are doing it the ground. This is a deeply realistic book for grown-ups, and I like that.

To conclude, this book is probably the best thing that can be read on this topic at this time. If you're in the voluntary sector, you can do a lot worse than invest two hours of your life to read it now, cover to cover. So turn off that phone, put the kettle on – and enjoy.

Craig Dearden-Phillips, Managing Director and founder of Stepping Out

Introduction

Collaboration should be an obvious and good idea for voluntary organisations. Getting organisations with similar aims and ethos to combine together in the interests of their beneficiaries or communities should be both logical and an opportunity to do something creative. However, collaboration is often perceived to be a threat where people fear that their organisation is being taken over or that it is losing its identity and original relevance.

Increasingly, collaboration (or more to the point, mergers) is promoted as a quick way of making savings. We need to challenge any fast rush to collaboration as a great cure-all. Our view is that collaboration is a longer-term strategy which, if done well, can create real value and difference.

Our objective was to pull together the practical experience of voluntary organisations that have experimented with different ways of collaborating from partnerships to joint agreements to mergers. In researching the book four factors were striking:

1. It is very easy to get lost in the technical detail of collaboration (designing structures, coping with constitutions and staff transfers) and to miss the important point: will collaboration make us more effective at delivering our mission?

2. Often the biggest obstacle to collaborative working is people's entrenched attitudes and reluctance to change. All too often we came across instances of rivalry, irrelevant competition of people unable or unwilling to see the bigger picture or how organisations working together can deliver more for their beneficiaries. Collaborating with others can pull us out of our comfort zone and challenge our complacency.

3. Collaboration is not a quick fix. The process needs time and careful planning to yield a return. Don't do it unless you are willing to put time into it.

4. The key factor in making it work is developing a culture that is open, being willing to learn from others and being able to move forward.

We would like to thank all of the organisations that agreed to share their experiences of what worked and did not work and we hope that this book will help to build strong and independent voluntary organisations.

Alan Lawrie and Jan Mellor

Acknowledgements

We are grateful to the following people and organisations for their permission to use case studies featuring their organisations.

Annie French (Leeds Advocacy Consortium), Prue Yeoman and Andy Brown (Manchester Citizens Advice Bureau – One Stop Shop), Mandy Forrest (Sheffield Well-Being Consortium), Alison Gibbon and Rachel Howley (Liverpool Specialist Advice Services), Dai Powell (Hackney Community Transport) and Karen Bowen (Cumbria CVS).

Chapter one
Why collaborate?

Sooner or later in the life of a voluntary organisation, the issue of how to work with similar organisations crops up. It becomes harder to explain the differences between what you do and what someone else does. Organisations with similar or even identical aims start competing for funds, resources and profile.

At one level, everyone can sign up to the idea of working in partnership. Working together sounds like a logical and sensible proposal. However, the nature of the discussion can change when somebody, often a funder, starts mooting the idea that there are too many organisations all doing the same things, and asks, would it not be better (or cheaper) if they all merged?

Over the last ten years, public policy towards the voluntary sector has pushed the idea of collaboration, by either including voluntary organisations in partnerships or encouraging organisations to work together.

This book sets out practical guidance on how small to medium-sized voluntary organisations can find effective ways of collaborating and working together in the interest of their users and communities. It is not just about mergers. Mergers are one way in which collaborative working can happen. There are several other ways of cooperating that can bring about benefits which are less final than a merger. The book aims to take an objective look at how voluntary organisations can develop ways of working together, based on practical experience drawn from throughout the UK.

This chapter starts with a quick exercise to identify what sort of attitudes towards collaborative working exist within your organisation, and explores what can motivate an interest in collaboration. It then looks at different models and formats for collaborative working, suggesting how trustees and managers can promote a positive process which leads to better services and outcomes for a voluntary organisation's users and community.

Exercise: isolation, rivalry or collaboration

Which ones do you recognise?

Attitude:	Isolation	Rivalry	Collaboration
Description	Stress is placed on what makes the organisation different from others.	The organisation wants to establish or maintain a leading position in its market.	Committed and open to work with others to achieve its mission.
Style	Emphasis on being a niche player, a specialist organisation and on protecting the organisation's 'territory.'	Focus on winning and being competitive. Often keen to grow and expand.	Flexible. Open and willing to invest in building relationships.
Organisational mantra	'We are different.' 'That wouldn't work here.' 'We are unique.'	'It's a jungle out there.' 'We compete to survive.'	'2 + 2 can make 5.' 'It is about win-win solutions.'
Management focus	Strong organisational culture. Sometimes very defensive to external developments.	Ensuring that the organisation is competitive, businesslike and able to win.	Outward-going. Keen to explore possibilities and open to change.
Risk factors	Danger of being inward-looking and over-defensive so it loses out on potential opportunities.	Losing the competition for funding. Being short-term. Focused on targets.	Spending a lot of time trying to build collaboration that does not lead anywhere.

What drives collaboration?

The need for voluntary organisations to work together can come from a variety of motives and driving forces. Some are what we have called 'push' factors where the need and commitment to work together is instigated from within the organisation. Collaboration is seen as a good thing that will help the organisation be stronger and enable it to meet its mission. Others are 'pull' factors. Pull factors happen when the organisation is pulled into working collaboratively by external factors and demands.

Common push factors

Finding better ways of delivering your aims

By collaborating, an organisation might find more effective ways of meeting its needs and objectives. This is often referred to as synergy. In organisational terms, synergy is when two or more things come together to produce a result not independently obtainable. So, for example, two organisations with different skills and expertise might be able to unite and deliver a result greater than their individual efforts because they have been successful at combining their resources.

Avoiding destructive competition

Cooperating on a formal basis stops destructive competition. Organisations work against each other's and users' interests by competing against one another on the basis of who can do it cheapest rather than who can deliver the best outcomes. Working together could stop this sort of destructive competition.

Sharing expertise and specialism

By teaming up, organisations may find ways of sharing expertise and specialisms. Collaboration might lead to the exchange of skills and learning between organisations.

Overcoming isolation

The process of working together might enable organisations to think more strategically, see opportunities and be less narrow or isolated.

Creating better service design and delivery

Collaborative working may be an opportunity to improve how services are designed and organised. It might lead to more accessible services for users, better coordination of services and ending some of the boundaries that might have grown over time.

Giving new focus

Working together may give the organisations a new focus, stronger identity and higher profile. Collaboration can be a positive way of relaunching or restarting an organisation.

Becoming a bigger and stronger player

By joining forces, organisations may be more competitive and win bigger contracts. It may make organisations more attractive to commissioners and funders, as they will have moved onto a bigger scale and developed a more resilient management infrastructure.

Case study: what's the alternative?

The manager of a health charity described how collaborative working became a key strategic issue for her organisation.

There are three other organisations which provide a similar service to us within a twenty-mile radius. We all struggle to keep going. It is getting harder as budgets get tighter and we are expected to do more. All four organisations have managed to work together and present a common front.

We are now actively looking at how we might collaborate more – up to and including merging. What has prompted this was not just noises from funders that we should cooperate to save money, but rather the thought that the way we are now isn't sustainable. We can't realistically continue as four proudly separate organisations all doing their own things, occasionally bumping into each other, bidding to the same people for declining resources. As managers we spend all of our time just about coping and keeping our organisation running. If we work really hard we might be able to keep our organisations going for a few more years, but it will be an exhausting struggle.

By finding a way of formally working together we hope to find a way of being stronger and more sustainable. We need to highlight the positive gains collaboration could bring, such as being able to free up time to do more strategic work and sharing practice across organisations. The alternative scenario is a grim one of four organisations all declining and struggling to keep going in splendid isolation from each other. To move it forward we need to build a very positive atmosphere about a vision for collaboration rather than seeing it as something that we will fall into as a last option when all else fails.

Common pull factors

Concerns about duplication

Funders often directly or indirectly imply that too many independent organisations are duplicating effort and that this is not the most efficient way of using limited resources.

A difficult market

Organisations frequently resort to working together in cases where their market is shrinking and getting tougher.

Preference for a single provider

Funders and commissioners may indicate that they prefer to deal with bigger or fewer organisations. Some funders find bigger organisations easier to deal with and have a view that larger organisations are a safer bet.

Survival

Safety in numbers: in tough times collaboration can be seen as the best survival strategy. In some cases, working with other organisations might be the only way of being able to continue in business.

Cost savings

Collaboration may reduce some organisational costs by sharing resources or reducing duplication of effort.

The threat of takeover

The move to work collaboratively is often provoked by a fear of being taken over or swallowed up by a bigger organisation.

Push/pull factors: a summary

Push factors: positive factors driving greater collaboration

- 'Cooperating on a formal basis stops us from destructive competition.'
- 'By working together we could share expertise and specialisms.'
- 'By joining forces we could be more effective than working in isolation from each other.'
- 'Our boundaries don't make sense. Working together could create better services for our users.'
- 'Working together could give us a new focus, stronger identity and higher profile.'
- 'By pooling our resources we could be more competitive and win bigger contracts.'

Pull factors: factors pulling an organisation into collaboration

- 'Our funders keep implying or saying that we are duplicating effort. They only want to fund one organisation.'
- 'The market is shrinking and getting tougher.'
- 'Collaboration looks like the best survival option.'
- 'Coming together could reduce some of our costs.'
- 'If we don't do it now on our terms we will get taken over by bigger organisations.'
- 'Our funders/commissioners have indicated that they prefer to deal with bigger or fewer organisations.'
- 'We are too small on our own to be viable.'

A critical issue for boards and managers is to ensure that everyone in the organisation (staff, volunteers, supporters and service users) understands the factors that are driving collaboration and appreciates the external context in which the organisation is operating. Collaborative working that is based purely on pull factors is unlikely to create real gains and value, as there is unlikely to be the genuine and long-term commitment to make it happen.

Competition

Competition between organisations can be a positive or a negative force. It can provide the motivation to challenge complacency, innovate and improve services. Negative competition can create waste, turn organisations against each other and prevent the potential gains that working together can bring.

A newly appointed trustee of a charity commented:

I have spent all my working life in the commercial sector in deeply competitive organisations where everything was about winning and beating the opposition. I came into the voluntary sector to get away from that and to do something useful. I am surprised at how much competition there is. It is often 'below the surface'. Although we talk about partnerships, shared goals and working together, we are very reluctant to share ideas and experiences with similar organisations doing the same work. Sometimes I think that we pretend to want to work together, but really there are very deeply engrained rivalries and suspicions of others. As the funding climate gets tougher my worry is that hidden competition will increase at a time when we should really be uniting.

Collaboration: giving up to get

Choosing to collaborate with another organisation should yield some gains. However, in order to collaborate successfully it might well involve organisations having to give up certain things, including:

- **Autonomy:** being able to do things on your own. In a collaborative working arrangement, an agreement or consensus will be needed between partners on some issues that previously individual managers or organisations could do or decide upon independently.

- **Speed of decision-making:** working in a collaborative venture or a partnership can take time. People have to be consulted, a consensus might take time to emerge and decision-making might be slower.

- **Your way of doing things:** collaboration usually involves agreeing to work in a similar or consistent way. Being part of a bigger venture might mean that individuals have to work in a more uniform and standardised way and have less capacity to do something in the way that they prefer.

In choosing to enter into a collaborative venture with another organisation it is important to recognise and acknowledge what you might have to give up. Hopefully what you give up will be replaced by clear and tangible benefits that can come from being part of a bigger venture.

Starting points

To get the process going, the following starting points are useful in exploring and developing ideas for organisational collaboration:

Start outside: look at the external landscape

The decision to work with another organisation is a key strategic one. Managers need to take time and study how the organisation's landscape might change and develop. It is useful to consider how key trends such as government policy, demographics, market development and changes in ways of working might impact to see if collaboration with other organisations would be a better and stronger position to respond from.

Focus on what will be the real gain to the user

The crucial test of any collaborative venture is whether it will lead to real and sustainable gains for the users or communities that the organisations are set up to benefit. How will collaboration benefit clients and communities? What positive short-term or long-term difference might it make?

Think strategically

The collaborative process takes time. Organisations need to be willing to invest time and resources in exploring options, testing possible models and in negotiating what can be a complex change. The gains and payback are likely to be in the medium term.

Build on strengths

A useful way of exploring the idea of working collaboratively is to identify the specific strengths that each potential player could bring to any new venture. Potential strengths might include specific skills or expertise, a track record or reputation or experience in a particular area of work. Identifying such strengths might be a way of spotting potential gains (or 'synergies' as they are called in management speak). The process of discussing and identifying strengths can lead to a much more positive and creative approach to collaboration, as it starts from a strong rather than a defensive position.

Manage the detail

Often in organisational-change projects, relatively small points or details grow and block the process. It is important that managers focus first on the reasons for collaboration and how it might ensure and assist the organisation's mission and then move on to detailed consideration of structures and people's roles.

Manage and lead the process

The process of exploring collaborative working needs to be navigated. The trustees and managers of all the parties must be committed to exploring it fully and willing to put time into it. The processes for consulting and involving staff, clients and other stakeholders need to be clear. The responsibility for making decisions must be understood. Expert and independent help might be needed on technical issues involved in change and in creating new structures (such as drafting new governing documents or transferring staff and assets).

Create a culture of open communication

All the parties need to be willing to talk openly about their interests, plans and concerns about future collaboration. Hidden agendas (ulterior motives, game-playing and holding things back) can very easily distort and delay progress. Work will also need to be done to ensure that users, supporters, funders and other stakeholders understand what is being discussed and are kept in touch with developments. Most organisations have an internal grapevine that can circulate rumours, news and disinformation faster than any official briefing system.

⚙ Case study: Springwater – starting with the big picture

The discussions at the two-day management retreat had been grim and sober. The trustees and managers of the Springwater environmental charity had met to discuss future strategy and to look at what options might be available to them. Sam, the chief executive, started the event by setting out the key issues on the organisation's landscape. Based on her experience she identified five key issues:

1. A much tougher funding climate. In the past, Springwater had been successful at raising funds from donors, trusts and a loyal supporter base. Sam produced evidence to show that funding was getting harder and that Springwater could not rely on past strategies. It needed to develop a new funding model and diversify its income base.

2. Greater competition. Sam identified 18 organisations that did (or claimed to do) similar things to Springwater. Several of them were newly created organisations set up to do things which were already being done! Sam had tried to work with some of them, but felt that the difficult funding climate was creating an atmosphere of distrust and rivalry.

3. Organisational size. Springwater had grown rapidly and now employed 20 staff operating at three locations. Sam felt that the organisation was at an 'awkward size': 'We are no longer a small organisation, but lack the resources in areas such as fundraising, technology and human resources to scale up to a bigger size.'

4. More opportunities. On a more positive note, Sam reported that there was no shortage of ideas for how Springwater could expand and also a regular series of invitations to develop in other areas.

5. A confused marketplace. Sam concluded by referring to her previous work as a marketing manager. She felt that Springwater's market was confused. She described what different organisations did, what they offered and that how they operated was completely chaotic. It was based on historic developments and ad hoc planning. She explained that funders, supporters and potential volunteers were often confused and could not understand how things fitted together. Sam felt that the situation was unsustainable and that there was a real danger of organisations collapsing into each other.

After some questions and debate, the trustees and managers discussed the best way that Springwater might move forward. They discussed different options and where the organisation might want to be in three to five years. After much deliberation and thought, the meeting agreed to ask Sam to sound out similar organisations about the possibility of exploring ways of collaborating, up to and including group structures and mergers. The group also agreed a 'communication line', setting out the message to go back to staff and supporters. It stressed how any possible collaboration was a positive and proactive move about strengthening Springwater and putting it into a stronger position to do its work.

After the management retreat, Sam organised a report-back session for staff and made contact with potential partners. As a result of this, Springwater is now involved in two jointly managed campaigns, is developing a social business with another organisation and is about to commission a feasibility study on exploring shared back office functions.

Sam commented:

I have learnt a lot from the exercise. We could only make progress because people could see how our external environment was shaping up and that staying as we were was not really an option. We had to do a lot of work to help some trustees and some staff understand the context we were working in and what the future held. I had kind of assumed that people would know and appreciate the bigger external picture, but that was not the case.

Once we agreed that 'business as usual' was not an option we had to convince people, both internally and externally, that collaborating and linking up with others was a positive and creative thing to do and not something we were being forced into. I think that because we were strategic about it and did it on our terms it has been a much more effective process. We were in the driving seat.

Barriers to working together

Organisations working together usually sounds like a good and logical idea. However, collaborative initiatives often get stalled, delayed or fall apart. From our observations of different attempts at collaboration, we identified eight common factors that can block it.

1. Personalities and ego

Collaborative efforts frequently fail because key people in leadership and management positions are reluctant to share, consider change or see the bigger picture. Often they find it easier to compete than to cooperate and collaborate.

2. Culture

Organisational culture is made up of all the traditions, history, style and 'ways we do things' that glue an organisation together. Cultures can be so strong that they block change and lead to an organisational mindset that is overly defensive and protective of how things are. For organisations to work together successfully there needs to be a culture that is open to change, willing to learn and open to new ideas, new people and ways of working.

3. A history of conflict among key interests

Past disputes, disagreements and rivalry can often linger and have an effect on the present. The director of a housing agency described how history affected current relationships with a neighbouring organisation doing similar work:

Years ago my predecessor fell out with the person who was their manager. It is hard to establish what the conflict was about, as all the people involved have moved on. But the level of suspicion and distrust has carried on. So we don't collaborate, share information or work together. On reflection, it is surprising how it has been allowed to continue.

4. Lack of obvious gain

Proponents of any type of collaboration need to make clear how they expect it to benefit the user and how it will enable organisations to do what they cannot do now. In short, it must show how any collaborative venture will lead to better services that will lead to real outcomes for users and communities. Without a clear case to show how collaborative working is likely to add value or put the organisations involved in a stronger position, it is hard to build up any real enthusiasm for it.

5. Technical issues block progress

Collaboration can involve a whole range of detailed organisational and managerial issues. Processes need to be established for sharing resources and budgets. Lines of accountability must be clearly agreed. Trustees need to feel that they are meeting their legal obligations to ensure the proper governance and stewardship of their organisation. More formal arrangements such as mergers can involve detailed consideration and negotiation of staff and resource transfers.

6. Lack of an effective process

As in any change process, managers need to ensure that people are kept informed and that the process for consultation and making decisions is clear. The process needs to engage trustees, staff, volunteers, supporters and users of all the organisations involved. However, it must also be efficient and make progress. All too often discussions about joint working drag on, fail to reach a conclusion or run out of steam.

7. Unfair distribution of responsibility and risk

In shared ventures it is important that each party knows what is expected of them and that there are clear rules and responsibilities. In collaborative exercises such as joint partnerships, it is often the case that one or two parties end up taking on all of the practical tasks needed to start and keep the partnership functioning. This blocks communication and causes resentment.

8. It is seen as a takeover

Joint working is often seen as leading to one organisation taking over another, even when reassurances to the contrary have been made. An organisational takeover is often perceived as a 'win-lose' situation. In some circumstances, the collaboration is a takeover; for example, where one organisation is in serious danger of collapse and is rescued by another. In these circumstances it is probably best to be honest and open about the reality of the situation. In others it is important to build respect between parties and avoid it being a power battle.

Options for collaborating

In considering ways of collaborating there are a number of different formats and options available to consider. Chapters 3 to 8 explore each option in detail, and describe what each is and the steps involved in setting it up.

In outline, there are nine possibilities, as shown in figures 1.1 to 1.9.

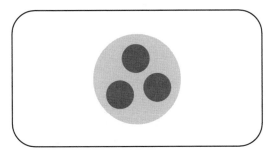

Fig. 1.1 Alliances: organisations stay independent but agree voluntarily to share information, support each other and work together to influence policy possibly under a common identity or umbrella.

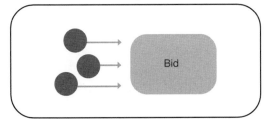

Fig. 1.2 Joint bidding: rather than organisations bidding for contracts in competition, they jointly bid for a contract. Responsibility for delivery and management must be clearly allocated in the bid.

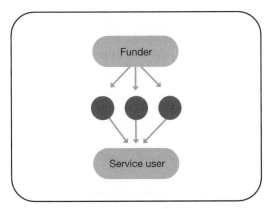

Fig. 1.3 Joint delivery: organisations share responsibility for the management and delivery of a service. They share the work and apportion costs and resources.

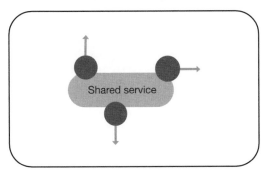

Fig. 1.4 Shared services: organisations agree to jointly manage a function or post across their organisations. The shared service provides a shared resource for all the organisations involved.

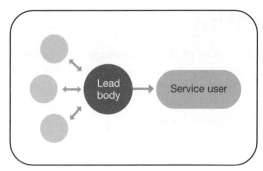

Fig. 1.5 **Lead body:** one organisation manages a project on behalf of other organisations. It is the responsible body for employing staff, finance and managing the service on behalf of the others. It acts as the managing agent. All of the participants should benefit from this joint management arrangement.

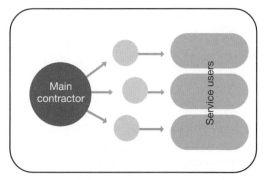

Fig. 1.6 **Subcontracting:** an organisation negotiates an agreement with another organisation to deliver a service. The other organisation might have skills, knowledge or resources that the main organisation lacks.

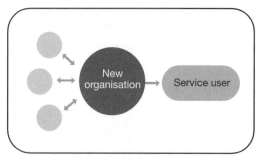

Fig. 1.7 **Consortium:** a new membership-based organisation is established to bid for and share work amongst the member organisations. The new organisation acts as the hub to win and oversee contracts and acts as a joint venture.

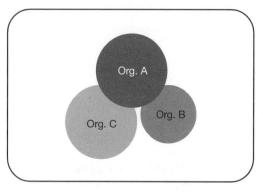

Fig. 1.8 **Group structure:** organisations join or merge and operate under a linked brand. Can be a federal structure or one in which one party has the governing role.

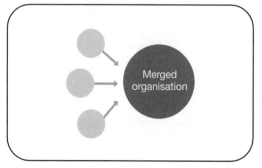

Fig. 1.9 **Mergers:** organisations combine together to become one organisation.

The following table elaborates on these collaborative formats, outlining what sorts of timescales are involved, in which instances any given format is helpful, and what the potential pitfalls or considerations are when getting into any given form of collaborative working.

	Outline definition	Timescale	Useful for:	Start-up/process issues
Alliances	Usually based on a voluntary agreement to coordinate and work together. Organisations remain independent.	Very flexible: can be formed around a specific issue or focus.	Speaking with a common or single voice. Campaigning work. Liaison and sharing information between organisations.	Can be very quick and informal to set up. Useful to develop ground rules as to how the alliance will work.
Joint bidding	Organisations remain independent, but agree to submit a joint bid for a project.	Needs time to develop the agreement and produce a bid.	Bidding for contracts to avoid organisations with a similar ethos bidding against each other.	May need to satisfy commissioners that any joint bid arrangements meet their procurement rules.
Joint delivery	Organisations remain independent, but agree to jointly deliver a service.	Can take time to establish relationship and negotiate an agreement between the parties.	Saving time on specific functions such as administration and back office costs by sharing resources.	Process needs to be carefully managed to ensure that the arrangements for delivering the work are watertight.
Shared services	Organisations agree to jointly manage and share a service that both need.	Often starts as an informal cooperative arrangement, but does need a clear structure.	Sharing 'back office' activities such as personnel management, computer support and other activities that organisations would struggle to provide on their own.	Need to ensure that the arrangement is tightly managed to avoid confusion. There may be VAT implications. *Cont.*

	Outline definition	Timescale	Useful for:	Start-up/process issues
Lead body	Organisations remain independent. Useful to have an agreement setting out the role and powers of the lead body and their responsibilities.	Usually set up to bid for and deliver a specific piece of work.	Delivering a programme or contract that involves different bodies. Bringing in smaller organisations.	Need to agree who the lead body will be and what powers are delegated to it. Need also to agree the relationship between the lead body and partners.
Subcontracting	One organisation contracts another organisation to carry out and deliver certain tasks for it.	Need to have clear agreement with expectations set out.	Subcontracting can be used to manage rises in demand or to bring in a particular expertise or skill.	It is usually regarded as a business relationship between organisations so could have implications for trading and VAT.
Consortium or joint venture	Usually involves establishing a new entity controlled by the partners to manage and/or deliver a particular function.	Medium- to longer-term. Organisations create and manage a new body to deliver a shared service.	Developing or delivering a major new programme or initiative that several organisations have an interest in.	Some work is involved in establishing a new body and agreeing how it will work.
Group structures	A business relationship between parties that they will operate under a common brand, but retain a level of independence.	A long-term commitment involving becoming a member of a group.	Smaller organisations accessing bigger contracts and drawing benefits from being part of a bigger group.	Often develops in an ad hoc way or as an alternative to mergers

Cont.

	Outline definition	Timescale	Useful for:	Start-up/process issues
Mergers	Organisations decide to wind up and either become part of another agency or to come together and create a new merged organisation.	As a long-term commitment, it is difficult to undo.	A major initiative.	Can be a complex process involving legal, staffing and management issues. TUPE (Transfer of Undertakings (Protection of Employment)) will apply if staff are being transferred (see page 120).

Four models of partnership-working

In a study on partnership-working, an Audit Commission management paper, *A Fruitful Partnership* (The Audit Commission 1998), identified four models of partnership-working for public agencies. These have been adapted to create the following table.

Model	Description	Potential advantages	Potential problems
A separate organisation is created.	A new organisation with a distinct and independent legal identity is created. The new body is able to employ staff and deliver programmes independent of the partners.	A clear and strong identity for the partnership. It might be able to do things that the individual partners could not do. A clear line of authority.	Is another structure really necessary? Partners could become distant from the new body and even see it as a rival for funding and profile. Can take time to set up.
The partnership is a virtual organisation.	The partnership does not have its own legal identity, but is housed by one of the partners. A lead or managing partner employs staff and manages budgets on behalf of the partners.	Relatively easy to set up. Does not require another structure.	Danger that the lead partner dominates or takes all the risk. Lines of accountability might be confused. *Cont.*

Model	Description	Potential advantages	Potential problems
Staff are co-located from partner organisations.	A less formal model. Staff from partner organisations work together to a common agenda and a common plan. Staff are employed by their organisation, but are encouraged to work together with staff from other partner organisations.	Focuses on practical collaboration at an operational level. Does not require another structure.	Can lead to confused reporting lines for staff. Depends upon trust and long-term commitment from senior management.
A steering group operates without dedicated staff resources.	A steering group operates and is made up of representatives of partner organisations. As a partnership, it does not have staff or budgets so any output has to happen through the partner organisations. It can sponsor, coordinate and encourage joint working.	Focuses on coordination across existing boundaries. Does not require another structure.	Depends on steering group members being able to get commitment and change back in their organisation. Can be short-term: depends on goodwill.

Can collaborative working fix it all?

While there can be many benefits of getting organisations to work together, it is not a panacea. There is a tendency for collaborative working (most often as a merger) to be suggested as a solution whenever an organisation hits hard times or is unable to make progress or transform itself. In this way, collaboration is often offered as an easy fix.

Our experience suggests that there is a danger of over-exaggerating the benefits that collaborative working can bring in the short term. Working together, partnership ventures or mergers will not by themselves solve problems such as poor performance or major funding gaps. Indeed, all that might happen is that the problem moves into a bigger scale.

As one manager we talked to put it, 'Putting two dodos together doesn't usually produce an eagle.'

Chapter two
The collaborative working process

This chapter looks at how voluntary organisations can usefully and creatively explore collaborative working and suggests some ways in which the process can be managed and led.

Collaboration can be a major event in the life of an organisation and as such it involves change. Change can very easily cause uncertainty, anxiety and stress within the organisation. The process can take time and needs careful stewardship for it to work. The way people are involved in the process can often determine the eventual success of the change process.

It is important to get the process in perspective. A major initiative such as merging with another organisation or creating a joint venture should involve detailed consideration and discussion. Other collaborative initiatives, such as setting up an alliance of like-minded organisations to campaign together, can be much more fluid and need only a simple working arrangement to give them order and structure.

First steps

The following exercise is a useful strategic first step to survey the current landscape and map out which organisations you might collaborate with, or even compete against, in the future.

Exercise: identifying potential collaboration

This exercise is designed to:

● help identify current and potential collaborators;
● take stock of the current relationship and future possibilities.

The first task is to make a list of all the organisations that have some significant similarities to yours in your immediate environment. This could include doing similar work or targeting the same users. Usually there are no organisations that are identical to yours, but there are some that overlap with you.

List below organisations to compare against	In what ways are we similar?	In which ways are we different?	Any current or past joint working?	What is the relationship currently like?	Future possibilities

Once you have identified similar organisations, move onto analysing respective similarities and differences and potential areas for cooperation and future joint working.

The exercise can be a very effective way of mapping out how different organisations have developed, highlighting areas of duplication or gaps and suggesting opportunities for working together.

Analysis

Could greater collaboration deliver better outcomes for our users and communities?

How much do we know about other people doing similar things to us?

What might be the first steps in exploring collaborative working?

Winners and losers

This quick exercise is a useful way of testing out the potential of collaboration. Take a look at the examples in the 'possible gain' and 'possible loss' columns and rate the possibility of each example coming to pass on a scale of 1 to 4. Add any other relevant factors to your list.

Possible gain	1: unlikely 2: viable 3: probable 4: highly likely	Possible loss	1: unlikely 2: viable 3: probable 4: highly likely
Able to deliver more services to our users and communities		Loss of identity and ownership	
Users better able to access services		Costs rise	
Better services		Loss of goodwill	
Savings in overhead costs		Danger of being too big – remote and inflexible	
A bigger profile		Process could be unsettling	
Better value for money		Danger of becoming impersonal	
In a stronger position to follow up future opportunities		A lack of skills to manage a larger organisation	
Sharing skills, specialisms and expertise		Loss of focus or specialism	
A stronger position to win funding and bids		Loss of autonomy	
A more sustainable organisation		Unsustainable in the long term	
Other:		Other:	

Analysis

Which of these factors need further exploring?

Are any of these factors major issues – deal breakers?

Creating the right conditions for collaborative working

Our research for this book found that a critical issue is getting the atmosphere right in the organisations concerned. Collaboration needs to be seen as a positive development that an organisation has chosen to go into with the aim of making it stronger and better able to meet its purpose.

All too often we came across examples of organisations feeling that they had been dragged into discussions because they had to rather than because they wanted to. Trustees and managers have a key role to ensure that they look at possibilities in a strategic and objective way and do not feel that they are being pushed into something which they can see little benefit of. Even if collaborative working is pushed onto the agenda (by, say, funding issues) it is important that organisations seize it and make sure that it is they who are driving and controlling it.

To create successful collaborative working arrangements, managers need to deal effectively with a range of 'hard' and 'soft' issues. Hard issues are easier to define. They are usually objective and tangible, are often about doing things properly, and need attention. Soft issues are about 'people' factors and how the process of building collaboration is managed.

Typical hard factors include:

- Legal considerations
- Financial implications
- Structures
- Technology and ways of working
- Personnel policies
- Risk analysis

Typical soft factors include:

- Management and governance style
- Organisational culture
- Commitment to collaborative working
- Ownership and involvement
- The way collaborative working will be introduced
- Relationships and style

The hard factors are easier to negotiate and plan for in a collaboration exercise. The soft factors are often hard to define, but are usually critical to success. If they are not dealt with, they are inclined to surface later in the process and can block progress.

With this in mind, managers need to discuss how the process of exploring collaboration will be organised and managed before getting into the detail of designing the collaborative working arrangement.

The following seven steps, which include various exercises and examples, can help the process.

1. Formally agree to open discussions

In many instances, the possibility of collaborating is talked about informally between parties. The discussion ebbs and flows, but is never formally resolved. It is useful to move the process on by parties agreeing to enter formally into discussions and start to test out what might be possible.

It can help to clarify issues and get things off to a good start if all the organisations involved publish a short joint statement setting out their intention to explore collaborative working, outlining the process and timetable and how people can contribute to the process. Such a statement can help to ensure that everyone gets the same message and reduce rumours and anxiety. The following exercise will help to get things started.

 Exercise: ten starter questions between organisations

These ten questions are intended to provide discussion prompts between organisations to aid the process of exploring collaborative working.

1. Why are we having this discussion?

Why is collaboration on the agenda?

Who or what is driving it?

2. What's on the horizon?

What's in the pipeline?

What are the issues and demands that we might have to cope with?

3. How do we work together currently?

How do we formally collaborate?

Are there any existing elements of informal collaboration?

4. Why can't we stay as we are?

What's wrong with the status quo?

Is change really necessary?

5. In what ways are we similar?

What do we have in common?

6. In what ways are we different?

How would you describe our differences?

7. What value might closer collaboration bring?

What might we be able to do together that we can't do separately?

8. What risks might be involved?

What could be lost?

What could go wrong?

9. What would successful collaboration look like?

What's our vision?

Describe possible models

10. How can we best take this conversation forward?

Who needs to be involved?

How do we plan the process?

2. Set up a task/steering group

A useful way to coordinate and carry out the exploration process is to set up a joint group made up of equal numbers from all of the interested parties. This group should have the responsibility of testing out what might be possible, develop options and then report back to their respective organisations.

It should not make decisions, but rather its role is to develop and test out ideas. It can be helpful to give the group a clear time limit for it to carry out its work to prevent the issue from dragging on. A sample terms of reference for a steering group is set out in the following example.

Draft terms of reference

This is an example terms of reference for a working group established between two voluntary organisations to explore the viability and potential of greater collaboration.

Collaboration Working Group

The ABC Charity and XYZ Voluntary Organisation (the parties) agree to establish a joint-working group to investigate the feasibility of greater formal collaborative working between them.

The membership of the group

The working group will consist of three members nominated by the ABC Charity and three members nominated by XYZ Voluntary Organisation. The group's meetings will be chaired on an alternate basis by the parties.

Terms of reference

The terms of reference are as follows:

To prepare an option and information report on the potential gains of and possible format for greater collaboration between the parties.

Tasks

The working group will undertake:

1. a study of existing forms of collaborative working that currently operate between the parties;

2. a review of the potential gains and costs of greater collaboration with regard to:

   - the impact of the services offered to clients and communities;
   - potential savings and any additional expenditure;
   - staffing and volunteer opportunities;
   - likely external opportunities and threats.

The working group will prepare a report to be presented to the trustees of both organisations within four months of the establishment of the working group.

Ways of working

Both parties agree to make available to the working group such reports, documents and financial information about their organisations as are useful and that do not breach either client or commercial confidentiality. Working group members agree to treat any material as confidential.

Members of the working group are not able to make commitments, policy or agreements on behalf of their organisation.

3. Ensure that trustees understand their role

The trustees are the governing body of a voluntary organisation and as such they have a legal duty to ensure the efficient management of the organisation and to safeguard its assets. Trustees need to be involved in the process and ensure that any new arrangements are within the organisation's legal powers and in the organisation's best interests.

The following exercise outlines key questions that trustees need to be asking. Major collaborative initiatives such as joint working, creating joint ventures and mergers cannot be delegated to staff or rubber stamped by trustees. At the start of the process trustees need to ensure that they understand the duties placed on them and how their organisation's governing document (memorandum and articles or constitution) expects them to work and to ensure that they have control over the process.

 Exercise: collaboration can be a major change project

It is important to approach collaborative working in a logical way. Why, what and how questions will usually crop up in any discussion. They need to be worked through in this order. People are often inclined to jump straight into the how questions: How will it affect my work or my job? How will we be organised? The whole process then becomes about detail rather than the more strategic questions involved in the Why and What questions.

Why?	Why are we talking about working collaboratively? (Avoid detail/focus on the bigger strategic picture and the likely external landscape.)
	Why are we being motivated/pushed to collaborate?

What?	What might collaborative working enable us to do that we cannot do separately?
	What benefits/gains might greater collaboration bring to our beneficiaries/ communities?
	What are the risks/what could be the downsides involved?
How?	How might we best collaborate? (Which organisational format (alliances, joint working, mergers, etc.) might deliver the best gain?)
	How do we manage the process?
	How do we develop a useful change process? (The implications for staff, volunteers and funders.)

4. Manage communications

In many organisations, the best way to make something public is for managers to try to keep it secret or to surround it in confidentiality. Rumours develop and the grapevine works fast. Managers need to ensure that staff, volunteers and users know what is being considered, why collaborative working is on the agenda and the process by which it is being explored. Work will be needed to ensure that a consistent message goes out to all at the same time.

Communication is not a one-way process. Managers must ensure that there are formal and informal ways for people to feed into the process and influence the discussion.

5. Involve stakeholders

Thought should be given to how to communicate and engage with external parties that have an interest or investment in the organisation. These might include:

● funders and commissioners;

● agencies that you work with;

● past and current supporters.

Experience suggests that informing them that discussions about collaboration are under way might lead to their positive involvement in the process. They might also be able to bring a useful external perspective to the process.

6. Consider external help for major collaborative initiatives

The work involved in testing out and developing a collaborative initiative can be considerable. It can also be difficult for one party to lead the process. There are advantages in finding an external and independent person to guide and facilitate the process. This could be met by finding a respected individual who might agree to lead the process or by engaging a consultant with expertise to aid the process. Such a person could oil the wheels, help with technical and expert tasks and even project-manage the collaborative process.

The following box describes the kind of role that a consultant could (and should not) play. Any such external help must be appointed by, managed by and acceptable to all of the parties. It can be useful to commission or carry out a feasibility study of a proposed collaborative initiative. Such a study can help to clarify issues and bring a level of objective analysis to the process.

Getting external help

Hiring a consultant can often bring an external perspective to a collaborative process or help to manage the process. Consultants can play several roles in collaboration:

1. **Feasibility.** A consultant can bring an independent view as to the feasibility and potential value of a collaborative initiative. They can take a more detached view and help to develop options, challenge assumptions and produce a feasibility study to inform discussions and decision-making.

2. **Facilitation.** A consultant can be used to aid the process. They can design and run meetings to ensure that issues are properly discussed and that people have the chance to contribute to and participate in the process.

3. **Technical advice.** Consultants should be able to give sound advice on the technical issues such as dealing with constitutional matters, employment issues, and organisational design that may be raised in the process.

4. **Project management.** A consultant can steer the process and coordinate the activities and work involved. Sometimes a consultant can be used as an interim manager to project-manage the formation of a collaboration venture.

In hiring and using external consultants it is important to be clear about the following:

1. **Who will the consultant be working for?** The consultant should be appointed by, accountable to and paid for by all the parties in the venture.

2. **Be specific about what you want them to do.** In drawing up the consultancy brief, be clear about what you want from the process. All too often a vague and unspecific brief leads to vague, unspecific and often expensive reports which tell you little that is new.

3. **What specific skills and expertise do you want the consultant to bring to the process?** Work out what sort of consultant you need and want. Is it a technical expert or do you need someone with strong process and facilitation skills to navigate the process?

4. **A consultant cannot make decisions for you.** A consultant can only advise, they cannot make the decisions for you or ensure that an initiative will work. The organisations involved must retain ownership of the process and the responsibility for making it work.

Finding a consultant

Useful sources of consultants working in the voluntary and community sectors are:

- **MDN**: The Management Development Network is a network of experienced freelance management consultants who work primarily or exclusively with voluntary organisations. MDN will circulate details of consultancy opportunities to its members. Contact: mdn@mdn.org.uk;

- **NCVO**: The National Council for Voluntary Organisations publishes an annual directory of approved consultants. Contact www.ncvo-vol.org.uk.

7. Manage and direct participation

The collaborative process needs to involve people and ensure that they are able to contribute to and shape the process. At the same time, the process needs to make progress and ensure that issues are resolved. All too often, the practice of consultation involves endless meetings that never reach a conclusion or consensus. Managers need to ensure that the process for involving people is planned and properly steered. From the outset, people need to understand the process, the timescale and who will be making decisions and by when.

Case study: Let's call the whole thing off...

On paper it made perfect sense that the three local organisations involved in providing services to young people should coordinate their activities and work together. They shared the same funders, had a similar user group and, on paper at least, had a similar vision and ethos.

The idea of working together had often been raised, but had never really progressed. A major breakthrough took place during the lunch break at a local conference. The chairs of the trustees and the three organisations' managers happened to sit together. During an informal discussion, several ideas for working together emerged. From this informal meeting they went on to meet on a more formal basis.

One of the participants described the process:

There was lots of quite ambitious and creative thinking at the first and second meetings. People floated ideas for running shared projects, employing a joint fundraising campaign organiser and developing common access points for young people. At first it all seemed very positive and exciting. However, things just never seemed to happen. To different extents, people were reluctant to give up total control and give one party the responsibility and authority to get on with it. Everyone wanted to have the last word on how it should be done. Although never said, there was a lack of trust. Looking back, there were a whole set of 'hidden agendas' that dominated our discussions – there was an unresolved conflict between two of the managers and a suspicion that one of the managers was empire-building and wanted to take everything over.

At our fourth meeting, it was obvious that, despite there being a logical case for working together, it just was not going to happen on any major scale. Key people were not up for it or prepared to set aside their negative feelings. It felt that we were trying to run before we could walk. In the end we agreed to meet formally three times a year to share experience and coordinate our future plans.

It's interesting that, although there was a strong and rational business case for collaborating, it was impossible without the personal commitment and leadership of key people in the three organisations.

Getting collaborative working on the agenda

At some point, the possibility of organisations working together needs to be evaluated and discussed on a formal and organised basis. It is better to discuss the issue proactively rather than to do it because you have to, either because funders are putting pressure on the organisation to do it or because of a crisis. Several factors can put collaborative working on the agenda:

1. Informal conversations/collaboration

After initially discussing the subject of working collaboratively, someone realises that it might be useful to agree to explore it formally. This often comes about when someone decides to grasp the nettle and propose that organisations spend time discussing it. It might also be discovered that informal collaborative working is already happening, as can be seen in the following case study.

Case study: informal collaborative working

It was a coincidence that both of the town's homelessness agencies had appointed new managers around the same time. In their first few months the new managers kept meeting up at local meetings and policy forums. After one such meeting one of the managers told the other that at her last board meeting the issue of joint working and collaboration had been raised. One of her trustees reported that he had had a discussion with a local commissioning manager who had tentatively said that it didn't seem sensible to have two organisations both doing the same thing but with little coordination or sharing of resources. Her board had asked her, as part of their strategic planning exercise, to explore ways in which the two organisations could collaborate and work together for a common goal.

The two new managers set about exploring forms and structures of potential collaboration. Their work changed after a casual conversation with the admin worker at one of the organisations. She had worked there for a long time and was surprised to find that the managers were spending time on this issue.

She explained:

> Our two organisations do work together; it's just that management doesn't really know about it! We regularly cross-refer clients if workers feel that the other agency is more appropriate. Workers often share specialisms and expertise, for example they have a worker who is brilliant at complicated housing benefit issues, so our workers regularly ring him if they need to check something out. We will often use each other's minibuses if they are over-booked or out of action. All of these arrangements are informal, lack any written agreement and have been built up by individuals over the years – sometimes despite the organisation!

Following this conversation, the two managers agreed that a good starting point was to acknowledge and support what was already happening rather than spend their time master-planning elaborate structures.

Exercise: collaboration – what do we do already?

This exercise is intended to help you identify ways in which your organisation currently collaborates and the forms of joint working that might have developed informally.

Type of collaboration	Your examples	How does it work? How is it organised?
Sharing resources		
Sharing expertise		
Policy work		
Users/clients		
Support		
Back office and admin		

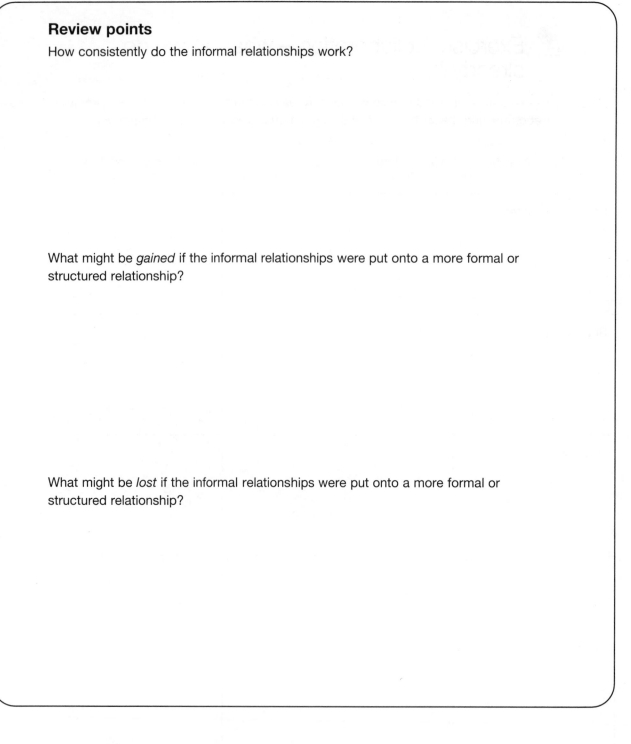

Review points

How consistently do the informal relationships work?

What might be *gained* if the informal relationships were put onto a more formal or structured relationship?

What might be *lost* if the informal relationships were put onto a more formal or structured relationship?

2. Funders and commissioners prompt it

Funders or commissioners will often express a view or preference that collaborating could be a good thing and might lead to better value. In this scenario, often 'collaborating' is seen only as being mergers and 'better value' is seen as cost reductions.

3. Opportunities arise

Through strategic planning and being in touch with the environment in which organisations operate, you can identify opportunities which could be approached better by working together rather than staying independent. Examples include opportunities to develop new services or to bid for significant contracts.

Exercise: future scenarios

Collaboration is often driven by external developments and trends. This exercise has three stages to it:

1. Identifying and predicting the trends and developments in the organisation's environment that are likely to be important and significant to the organisation. Trends might be positive or negative.
2. Once the trends have been identified you can then start to discuss and agree assumptions that you can draw about the likely prospects for your organisation over the next few years.
3. The final stage is to develop and draw different scenarios or options about how you might be organised in the medium to longer term to meet the key changes and trends.

Once the scenarios have been identified you can then agree which ones are worth developing and exploring further.

Stage	Questions	
1. Trend spotting	What's on the horizon for us? What are the likely key trends or factors that will have an impact on our organisation?	
2. Assumptions	What are likely to be the key challenges facing our organisation? What will we need to manage and respond to? What might be the same or different over the next few years?	
3. Future models	How might we develop? Which structures might be possible? How could we collaborate?	

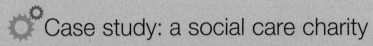

Case study: a social care charity

An established social care charity worked through this model and identified key trends, future business assumptions, and five possible future scenarios to work on.

Key trends

Decline in funding
Increased demands
Bidding for contracts
New legislation
Technology use
New policy
More competition
NHS changes
New commissioners
Interest in social enterprise
Personal budgets
Cuts in social care

Future business assumptions

Tougher climate
Continual change
Need to be strategic
Opportunities to collaborate

Possible scenarios: three to five years' time

1. More or less the same	2. Struggling to survive	3. Independent but connected	4. Independent but in formal agreements	5. Merged – part of a bigger and new organisation
Assume no real change or difference from what we do now. Our structures, services and role will probably still be relevant.	Tough times ahead. Fewer resources, and greater demand and competition. Clinging to our model and ways of operating. Hope that something turns up.	Still as we are but wired in to partnerships and alliances with similar organisations. Better coordination, strong links with others and working on joint activities.	Still independent but working with others through a range of joint ventures, partnerships and joint arrangements. Flexible organisation working in a variety of different ways.	Part of a bigger and new organisation with a new identity, profile and working on a larger scale.

4. Circumstances change

Internal developments in an organisation can often make collaborative working an option. In one charity the impending retirement of their chief executive made it easier to discuss big strategic issues such as a formal partnership with a similar agency.

5. A crisis occurs or is 'just about' avoided

Collaborative working is often seen as a way to strengthen an organisation and recover from a difficult time. The board of a community development organisation decided to look at ways of building partnerships after a particularly difficult funding round. Their Director commented, 'The board felt that things were getting harder and that each year we were struggling to survive. They asked me to develop options for collaboration as an alternative to continual crisis management.'

Commissioners'/funders' interest in collaboration

An increasing number of organisations have reported to us that commissioners have actively encouraged or prompted organisations to consider working together. Four factors seem to drive this:

- A belief that working together (up to and including mergers) will reduce organisational costs and create savings.
- A belief that having fewer organisations will reduce duplication and make commissioning easy.
- An implied preference for dealing with bigger organisations.
- A belief that collaboration could improve the service experienced by clients by having better coordination, less fragmentation and better joined-up delivery.

This push for mergers frequently causes interesting contradictions. 'Reducing duplication' could lead to having only one or two providers. How does having only one or two organisations capable of providing a service improve user choice? In some instances, the push towards mergers has created a position where there is a monopoly or near-monopoly of providers. It is useful to challenge concerns about 'duplication'. Is there a danger that the alternative could lead to a loss of choice, specialism and the commissioner being in the vulnerable position of being dependent on one main provider?

There is no comprehensive evidence that mergers create significant cost savings. Funders should really focus on the quality of the work delivered and its ability to create lasting outcomes for users and communities rather than attempting to direct the structures of the organisations with which they work.

It is worthwhile to involve funders and commissioners early in the process. They may have a perspective or understanding about gaps, future strategies and priorities that could influence decisions. Having them on board may well help to speed up the process and build a stronger relationship. It is also worth checking that funders do not have any procedural or funding and commissioning rules that could block joint working. For example, one local authority's standard procurement terms require potential bidders not to discuss or communicate their bid to any other party. Such a rule (brought in to stop bidders operating as a cartel or engaging in price fixing) makes partnership-working and joined-up thinking, which the authority also supports, somewhat difficult!

Identifying potential gains and losses

Most change processes involve some people gaining and some people losing. A clear case for collaboration should be made so that people can make a balanced decision whether to proceed. The case must set out the likely and possible gains and also the likely and possible losses. The following table outlines some potential losses and gains.

Possible gains	Description	Example
Able to deliver more services to users and communities.	Organisations are able to increase their capacity and use their shared resources to meet more needs.	By working together and coordinating plans, two training agencies were able to enhance their performance.
Users are better able to access services.	Collaborating can lead to a more joined-up service plan.	Three advice agencies agreed to coordinate opening times and use a common telephone number to increase access for clients.
Better services overall.	Collaboration can allow more up-to-date services that are built around best practice to be created.	Four local youth agencies developed a common set of quality standards and a shared improvement plan.
Savings in overhead costs.	Working together can reduce management and overhead costs by reducing duplication.	Two merged housing organisations were able to identify some savings by only needing one head office and by sharing management and overhead costs.
A higher profile.	Organisations can become higher-profile and have a greater influence on policy.	Three charities for people with disabilities felt that creating an alliance to lobby and campaign gave them a 'bigger and louder voice'.
In a stronger position to follow up future opportunities.	Organisations can become better able to tender and win contracts and other opportunities.	A newly merged community support agency found that commissioners preferred to deal with one larger organisation.
Able to share skills, specialisms and expertise.	Collaboration could lead to greater learning and development opportunities for staff.	By working together, two environmental charities were able to share practice and learn from a greater pool of expertise.
A more sustainable organisation.	Joining forces creates 'safety in numbers'.	The trustees of a children's charity felt that working in partnership with other agencies had reduced the potential for unhelpful competition and a reliance on only one or two income streams.

Possible losses	Description	Example
Loss of identity and ownership.	By becoming part of a bigger operation, local goodwill, contacts and closeness to users are reduced or lost.	By becoming part of a larger regional organisation, some staff of an educational venture felt that they were now perceived as 'out of touch and no longer local'.
Costs rise.	The costs of being bigger can increase disproportionately.	A newly merged organisation found that its overhead costs increased overall to meet the costs of being a bigger single organisation.
Loss of goodwill.	Some donors might no longer feel the same level of commitment.	An arts charity lost some long-established donors when it became part of a bigger venture.
Danger of being too big: becoming remote and inflexible.	'Bigger isn't always better.'	A trustee of a health charity felt that a collaborative structure slowed down the charity's responsiveness, as it needed to consult and engage with partners.
Process of collaboration could be unsettling.	The time involved in exploring collaboration is demanding and causes anxiety.	The director of a social care charity estimated that time spent debating a possible merger (which did not come off) had caused a lot of worry for staff and taken up considerable management time.

The governing document

A charity's governing document may be called its constitution, memorandum and articles of government or trust deed. The document will set out the legal aims and powers of the charity and describe who it is intended to benefit and in which locations. All activities should fit with the governing document. Most governing documents will not impede or prohibit your ability to work with others. It is important to check that any proposed collaborative venture is in line with the organisation's constitutional powers and aims.

In the case of a fundamental change such as a merger, the governing document will usually have a dissolution clause that sets out how the charity can be wound up and transferred to another body. If the governing document could limit your ability to operate in a collaborative way, it is important that you take expert advice on the best way to proceed or on how to change your governing document.

The following example suggests questions to ask trustees before considering collaborative working and summarises the points made above.

Key questions for trustees

Trustees have the individual and shared responsibility to safeguard a charity's assets and reputation. In considering any collaborative venture, trustees need to address the following questions.

Is the proposal in line with our legal aims and powers?

Any proposed collaboration needs to be compatible with the aims and objects set out in the organisation's governing document (often called the constitution, memorandum and articles of government, or rule book). The governing document will usually set limits on the kinds of activities a charity can carry out and often the geographical areas that the charity can operate in.

Are the risks involved reasonable?

All activities and initiatives involve some sort of risk. Possible risks might include:

- **Business risk:** the proposed venture might reduce our ability to generate income from some sources.
- **Organisational risks:** key staff and volunteers might leave.
- **Reputation risk:** if the venture fails it could damage our standing and reputation.
- **Financial risks:** the costs of setting up and running the new venture could be much more than predicted.
- **Political risk:** important stakeholders and supporters may not understand or like the collaborative venture and withdraw their support.

The purpose of discussing risk is not to arrive at an end point where any new project is risk-free and does not have any potential risks associated with it. Rather, the purpose is to ensure that the risks have been identified, that actions to reduce them or manage them are in place and that the trustees are comfortable with the level of risk involved.

Will the venture enable us to deliver our strategy?

Any potential collaboration must fit with the organisation's strategy. Hopefully the organisation has a strategy that sets out key priorities for the period ahead and gives a steer as to how the organisation would like to develop and change over the next few years. Any proposed strategic venture should fit with the organisation's strategy. A useful question to ask is what will collaborative working enable us to do in the future that we cannot do on our own?

What is the cost involved?

Trustees need to understand the full costs involved in any proposed collaborative venture. At an early stage it might only be possible to agree broad principles and to look at the overall assumptions and business case. Possible questions might include:

- What are the likely costs involved in setting this up?
- How much will we and other partners be expected to contribute?
- What about hidden costs (management and staff time spent on developing it)?

What's the alternative?

It is useful to look at the alternative to collaboration. Is keeping things as they are a realistic and sustainable option in the medium to longer term? Is there an opportunity cost involved (i.e. by not doing this we might lose out)? Could collaborating lead to a destructive and negative competitive relationship?

Are the other parties in the proposed initiative in a sound and proper state?

Trustees need to be sure that potential partners could not damage their organisational standing or reputation. Collaborating with an organisation with a poor business position or with a track record of poor delivery could be damaging and affect your reputation. There needs to be transparency between partners and a process of due diligence so that each partner knows what and who they are getting involved with.

What not to do

Seven ways to sabotage a discussion about potential collaboration

1. 'Have you thought about...?'

Focus on the detail. Insist that every aspect of the proposed collaborative effort is planned and organised before you can agree to proceed.

2. 'We need a full and comprehensive study on how the new structure will work in detail.'

Subject it to a detailed feasibility review. Demand that the idea be subject to a lengthy examination of every aspect that will lead to a detailed report being produced.

3. 'X won't like it.'

Blame someone else. Claim that a third party – users, volunteers or funders – will oppose it. Hide behind their assumed opposition.

4. 'We must make sure that everyone is fully consulted.'

Over-consult. Plan a detailed and time-consuming consultation exercise with everyone who comes in contact with the organisation. Spend ages consulting – people will get bored with it.

5. 'Apparently they have a dodgy reputation.'

Subtly attack the other party. Imply that the organisation you are considering collaborating with is failing, incompetent or different from yours and so could damage your reputation or brand.

6. 'Let's do another risk analysis'

Focus on the negative. Only talk about what you could lose from working collaboratively.

7. 'Our constitution/contract/funding agreement will make it impossible to do.'

Raise a technical or minor issue into a principle. Find a small sticking point and elevate it into a 'deal breaker'.

Chapter three
Alliances

This chapter looks at how organisations can stay independent but find ways of coordinating their activities and communicating with similar organisations.

What makes an alliance?

An alliance is an arrangement or partnership between two or more parties who determine that they have a shared ethos and interest and decide to work together in order to advance common goals and to meet common interests.

A key characteristic of an alliance is that all of the organisations remain independent. However, it can, if the alliance members want it to, lead on to other more formal and organised forms of collaboration.

Alliances can meet various needs, including:

- providing an organised forum for liaison, communication and sharing information between independent agencies;
- helping to overcome individual and organisational isolation by providing a place for people to share experience and learn from each other;
- offering an opportunity to develop a common or united front between organisations to influence policy and campaign for common goals;
- creating a forum for organisations to coordinate their activities, develop strategies and share future plans;
- encouraging cooperation and work against destructive competition within a sector;
- being the base from which other forms of collaboration are developed.

Examples of alliance-working

- A group of community workers working in the same locality meeting together to share experiences.
- A network of organisations involved in services for people with learning disabilities meeting together to coordinate input into the local authority's commissioning strategy.
- A partnership of arts agencies working together to run a joint audience development campaign.
- A group of mental health organisations coming together to run a campaign challenging perceptions and prejudice about mental health.

Creating a focus

A member of a successful alliance of local organisations working with people with a disability described how the alliance was established

The main driving force behind our success as an alliance was our local authority, who is also our main funder. Their permanent state of confusion and lack of any clear strategy created a strong and urgent need for organisations to come together. We needed to share information, develop a common voice, and see how we could best work together and help to shape policy. The local authority's failings acted as a real catalyst. We needed to work together and avoid individual organisations being played off against each other.

There needs to be a common bond that unites all members together. This might be:

- geography: organisations involved in a particular area meet together;
- provision of similar services or work with particular client groups;
- a common approach or ethos: organisations with a particular approach such as developing user involvement work together to share experience and support each other;
- a specific issue: groups come together to campaign or lobby for a particular (usually time limited) goal;
- a common objective: groups work together to run a specific activity jointly, such as an awareness campaign.

Alliances come about in a variety of ways. Often informal contact between organisations is firmed up and develops more of a structure and identity. Sometimes organisational alliances are created for a specific purpose, such as to campaign for or influence a particular issue. Some alliances are established to be ongoing, whereas others are much more temporary – they meet together to do a particular activity and when it is completed, they stop meeting.

Several established alliances seemed to work best when there was a clear and obvious focus for coming together. A member of an advice network in a Midlands town described his experience:

We started meeting formally a few years ago when the local authority announced a major review of advice provision. A couple of us thought that it would be useful to share information and try to work out our common position. Because we were dealing with a very live and important issue, our first few meetings were very well attended and had a real purpose. Once that issue faded, numbers attending dropped off and meetings lacked focus. However, we'll keep the network ticking over with regular meetings and we'll be ready for the next big issue to come along.

A good starting point is to try to establish what the common bond is between all potential alliance members. This might involve looking for a similar ethos or shared values; or, as one person commented, 'Although we all came from different organisations of a different shape, history and style, it came together when we worked out what we all stood for.'

Structures

An alliance need not have a formal organisational structure. Several options are possible, including:

- a group without any formal legal identity meets together in an informal way to discuss topics of mutual interest;
- an organisation (such as a local Council for Voluntary Service) agrees to convene the group and take responsibility for supporting its operation;
- one of the member organisations agrees to act as the point of contact for the group and to act as its secretary;
- the group adopts a constitution, elects officers and operates as a free-standing body with its own arrangements.

There is a danger in spending too much time on structure to the point where it stops flexibility and responsiveness. It is often pointless to create another structure that needs administrating, organising and servicing.

Making alliances work

The following ten points indicate how to develop effective ways of working with other organisations and include some examples.

1. **Work out what you stand for.** Do not assume that what you have in common is obvious. It is worth discussing bigger-picture issues such as organisational vision and values. Try to define the purpose of the alliance in terms of the benefits and outcomes it will bring to the user/communities.

2. **Agree a simple terms of reference or memorandum of understanding.** It is useful to draw up a simple agreement setting out the purpose of the alliance, how it will operate and what is expected of members. Such a document will be helpful in explaining the alliance to new or potential members. All members should be asked to sign up to it formally. This should not be a rubber stamping exercise; it should involve the trustees and managers in discussing how working through the alliance will help to support their organisations' goals.

3. **Be focused on what you are going to do.** Decide a few key priorities for the alliance. Don't aim to do too many things. The first few activities should be realistic, achievable and demonstrate the value of working together.

4. **Agree what you are not going to do.** It is important to be clear about what you are not going to do and which roles you will not play. A partnership of health projects found that stating the partnership would not 'employ staff, run direct services or bid for funds' helped to clarify people's understanding of its intended role and also to reassure people that the intention was not to 'build an empire to compete against what was already there'.

5. **Agree how you are going to work.** All groups need rules. This is particularly true of informal groups. It is useful to agree some basic rules about how the alliance will work and how members are expected to behave. Possible rules might include: respecting confidentiality and difference, how decisions will be made, how the alliance will be resourced and what happens if there is a disagreement between members.

Example: a memorandum of understanding for an alliance between organisations

Anytown Youth Organisations Partnership

Purpose of the agreement

This memorandum of understanding is intended to encourage and enable liaison, communication and collaboration between the parties to support the provision of high-quality services to young people in Anytown.

Parties

- Anytown Youth Group
- Youth Outreach Project
- New Horizons Group

Shared vision and values

All of the parties believe that sharing experience, plans and joint working will lead to stronger organisations and better services for young people.

All of the parties are committed to working in a way that is open, transparent and honest.

All of the parties are committed to creating and building services that reflect best practice and are:

- responsive;
- flexible;
- accessible;
- reflective of the diverse and changing needs of young people;
- involving and engaging of young people;
- effective.

Roles of the alliance

The alliance exists to:

- coordinate and support the delivery of high-quality services to young people in Anytown;
- coordinate and encourage collaboration between the partners;
- influence social policy and commissioning practice based on the experience of the partners.

To meet these aims the alliance will:

- share experience and develop practice between members;
- monitor and respond to policy;
- explore ways of collaboration between parties;
- encourage training and professional development between the staff and volunteers of the parties.

The alliance will not:

- apply or bid for funding contracts to run direct services;
- employ or manage staff.

Limitations of the alliance

The relationship between the parties is that of independent organisations and nothing in this agreement shall create or be deemed to create a partnership or relationship of agency, franchise, or employment between the parties.

No party shall enter into any contractual obligations on behalf of the other party, without the prior express written consent of an authorised signatory of the other party.

Membership

Membership is open to any independent voluntary agency operating in Anytown that provides services to young people and supports the core values of this partnership.

Organisational issues

The alliance group will be made up of the five chief officers (or their deputies). The alliance group's role will be to:

- coordinate the work;
- encourage joint working;
- monitor relevant policy development;
- represent the interest of youth agencies to statutory bodies.

One of the partners will act as the secretariat for this agreement. The role of the secretariat is limited to:

- convening and hosting meetings of the steering group;
- preparing and circulating agendas, and action notes;
- ensuring that any decisions are followed through;
- holding any funds on behalf of the alliance.

The alliance group may appoint or convene working or task groups to carry out specific projects. The membership and terms of reference for any group will be agreed by the chief officers group. Such groups should have a limited scope and timescale. The chief officers group will oversee the work of any project or task group.

All of the parties to this agreement are committed to:

- working in an open, honest and transparent way;
- consulting and involving other partners on any matter, project or bid that might have city-wide implications or opportunities;
- sharing experience, expertise and skills between partners;
- respecting the differences between partners;
- respecting confidentiality if requested to do so.

6. **Share the work around.** In any cooperative venture, it is important to ensure that one party is not allowed to monopolise the organisation or feels that everything is dependent on it. A style of work needs to be developed where tasks are shared between members and responsibilities for chairing and servicing meetings are regularly rotated between members. One tactic used by a housing alliance was to ensure that all tasks agreed by a meeting were written up during the meeting and responsibility for implementing them clearly allocated. 'This shows who is and who is not doing the work. The objective is that everyone has something to do, even if it is only a small job, as commitment to a group comes from doing things rather than attending meetings.'

7. **Be realistic.** A member of a network of care providers described how her network ran into trouble: 'We over-committed. People kept having good and useful ideas as to what we could do together. We never said 'no'. On reflection we set ourselves up to fail.' It is better to aim to do a few things well than to attempt to cover too many areas.

8. **Encourage sharing.** Effective alliances need to build up a culture or style of working that encourages sharing. This can be challenging. One experienced voluntary sector activist described their experience: 'Although we all say we are into working together, often there is a high level of mistrust and suspicion that usually is never formally expressed. It is interesting how people are reluctant to talk about their future plans and funding bids in case they give something away.' Breaking down such an atmosphere and building a more open culture will take time. One partnership designed its meetings so that every group did a regular session talking about their issues and future plans just to encourage openness.

9. **Respect difference.** Working together does not mean we all have to be and act the same. Acknowledgement and encouragement of difference is an important building block. A participant in an advice network described an important breakthrough as being 'the point when we accepted that there are several different ways to run an advice service. It need not be a discussion about how one way (i.e. my way) is best. From that point we were able to share experience and learn from each other.'

10. **Have occasional reviews.** To ensure that an alliance remains relevant it is worthwhile to schedule occasional review discussions to discuss how the alliance is developing and take stock of its progress. Discussion prompts for such a review topic are set out in the following exercise. It is also useful to go back to the original idea behind the alliance set out in the terms of reference and any ground rules as to how it should operate to check that they are still relevant and being adhered to.

Exercise: taking stock – measuring progress

This exercise suggests six key questions that could form the basis of a review session. The aim is to focus on what the alliance has achieved or contributed to, to recognise its value and agree future ways of developing it.

Discussion prompts for an alliance review session

What have we achieved?	What have we not done?
Why do I keep coming to alliance events and meetings?	If the alliance had not been in existence what would be missing?
What do we need to do more of?	What do we need to do less of?

Is it time to close?

There comes a point in the operation of an organisational alliance where its future needs to be reviewed. Be careful that the alliance does not just drift or gradually become dormant or moribund. Key signs, such as fewer people participating or attending meetings or the running of the alliance starting to feel like a chore or routine, might be the prompts to ask if there is still a point in carrying on or if the work of the alliance and the need for it could be done best in another way.

⚙ Case study: peaks and troughs

The convenor of a network of local training agencies reflected on her experience of being involved in running the network over ten years.

Levels of interest and membership have varied considerably over the years. Sometimes meetings have been packed out and the network has been really lively. On other occasions, only a few people turned up and we have had to struggle to find things to discuss.

Looking back, the network works best when there is an obvious point to it – such as coping with a new funding regime – this provides a focus to bring people together. When we don't have such a focus, we should put the network onto the back burner until it is needed again.

Ways to keep an alliance motivated and together

The following eleven ideas can be used to keep an alliance focused or to refresh it.

1. **Ask why people attend its meetings.** What do they hope to gain from it? What should it be doing?

2. **Rotate roles.** Develop a style of work where tasks such as chairing meetings, writing minutes and organising events are shared out amongst members rather than done by one or two.

3. **Avoid being in a rut.** Change the format of meetings to encourage variety.

4. **Learn together.** Get members to share their experience. Run study days to encourage learning from each other's practice.

5. **Acknowledge expertise.** Get members to identify what they are good at or specialise in and see if this can be shared across the alliance.

6. **Use social media.** Social networking sites such as Facebook can provide an easy and cost-effective way of organising a network and encouraging communication between members.

7. **Involve others.** Set up sessions for other groups such as trustees, fundraisers and admin staff in the alliance's member organisations to network.

8. **Swap and share skills.** Encourage secondments, job swaps and shadowing between staff to encourage learning.

9. **Set the agenda.** Use the alliance's collective experience of services to develop strategies on how you would like to see services develop.

10. **Celebrate the work.** Use the alliance to get media coverage of success stories and evidence of the difference you make.

11. **Benchmark.** Use the alliance to get members to compare their practices so that members learn from each other and get a different perspective.

Chapter four
Joint working

This chapter looks at three types of joint working:

1. **Joint bidding:** when organisations make a joint bid for funds or a contract to deliver a programme.
2. **Joint delivery:** when organisations agree to manage a project or programme of works jointly.
3. **Sharing services:** where organisations meet their needs by jointly managing a shared function or role.

Joint working between organisations to deliver projects has become a significant part of the voluntary sector landscape. Terms such as 'partnerships', 'joined-up thinking' and 'joined-up government' are now very much part of the sector's vocabulary.

Funders and government increasingly see working in partnership as a way of breaking down traditional barriers and, ideally, leading to a point where the sum of the parts is greater than the whole.

Advantages and issues

There are several advantages to joint working when partnerships work successfully, including:

- enabling smaller or specialist organisations to stay independent and still deliver on a bigger scale, by sharing skills and expertise;
- bringing together some interesting combinations or producing synergies that lead to more creative and stronger services;
- creating a more seamless service for users and communities owing to the sharing of work;
- generating better value for money, as organisations pool resources;
- stopping duplication and unhelpful competition.

However, creating effective joint-working arrangements can be fraught with difficulties. Are the organisations able to work together? What happens when things go wrong? Are the management and governance relationships clear? In addition, the motives for creating a partnership may need to be probed. One civil servant described working in partnership as being 'the temporary suspension of mutual hostility between organisations to get hold of project funding'.

The key issues which can emerge as organisations move into joint arrangements include the need to:

- examine the joint project critically to ensure that issues around governance, risk and accountability are clear;

- make sure that delivery and management arrangements are watertight and that the lines of accountability are clear;
- ensure that all parties are committed to and able to operate to the same standards and offer a consistency of service;
- have clear procedures and processes to resolve problems that might occur in the life of a joint project.

Examples of joint working between voluntary organisations

- Two organisations linking up to bid for a contract.
- Three health charities pooling resources to employ a policy and campaigns worker jointly.
- Six local organisations operating as a partnership to bid for and deliver a government regeneration programme.
- Two organisations combining efforts to run a new fundraising campaign.

Joint bidding

As voluntary sector funding increasingly moves into a bidding or contract culture, voluntary organisations, often with the support of public sector organisations, have tried to find ways of jointly bidding for and delivering services. In some instances, commissioners have accepted either joint or linked bids from organisations to deliver the same contract (see fig. 4.1). Organisations have also experimented with establishing new structures to bid for and manage services jointly.

An alternative structure whereby one party acts as the lead or managing body is outlined in detail in chapter 5. Chapter 6 describes how some organisations have developed consortia to combine effort and win bids.

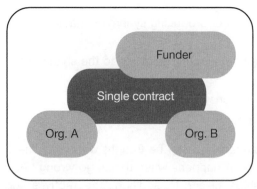

Fig. 4.1 A joint bidding model.

In the scenario shown in figure 4.1, the funder or commissioner has one funding agreement with two (or several) organisations. The organisations divide up the work between them. The organisations work together and share resources to achieve the intended outcomes.

If the decision is made to bid jointly, the organisations involved should develop an agreement or memorandum of understanding which sets out how they will cooperate (see page 46).

Bidding together is feasible, but is not without risks. The bid needs to show that there is a clear arrangement for dividing up the work and clear lines of accountability.

In negotiating such agreements, it is important to consider what could happen in the life of a joint bid and how the agreement would manage it. It is often useful to imagine worst-case scenarios and ask 'what if ...?' questions. Issues to focus on include:

- What would happen if one party in the joint bid failed to perform?
- How would problems or disputes be resolved?
- How do we keep our brand identity and relationship with the community if a service is being delivered by someone else?
- How would the end of the agreement be managed?
- How could we ensure a consistent quality across providers?

It is worth checking with key funders or commissioners to see if they have any concerns or issues about joint-working arrangements. One local authority commissioning manager described his concerns:

> We have had mixed experience of joint arrangements. The main concern of our legal and procurement people is to ensure that if something goes wrong it is obvious who we can take action against. Sometimes in partnerships it is hard to see who is really in charge.

Our experience in doing research for this book has shown that this model seems to be less popular now. This appears to be because both parties are jointly liable for the contract's performance and commissioners feel more comfortable with a single contract with one party.

Joint delivery

Over the past few years there has been a push from government to encourage organisations to work with other organisations and develop a real commitment to joined-up service delivery and partnership working. At the heart of this is breaking down compartmental thinking or 'silos', as they are often called, where services managers and staff do not see the whole picture or how things are from the client or user perspective.

Silo-thinking happens when the boundaries around services make them less effective. Users frequently do not fit into a neat and tidy pigeon-hole. The issues and problems which they have might cut across the way we choose to organise things. So, for example, a young person who is homeless may have a range of issues from finance, housing, education and addiction. Often they will spend their time being shunted around different agencies that all try to do their best in their area of interest, but no one, except the user, sees the whole picture.

Joint delivery is when organisations agree to stay independent, but they design, plan and implement ways in which services communicate better, coordinate their activities and deliver integrated services.

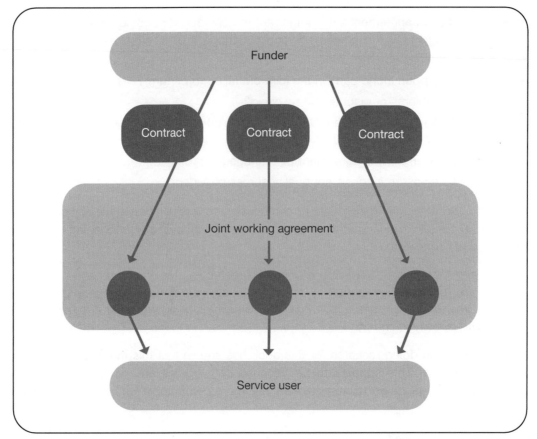

Fig. 4.2 A joint delivery model.

Joint delivery can take a variety of forms:

- Designing practical arrangements for referring clients between individual organisations.
- Producing common publicity materials.
- Operating from shared locations.
- Having a single point of entry to the service.
- Providing processes for users to move between services seamlessly.
- Operating services to the same quality standards.
- Having staff able to work together with complementary skills and expertise.

At the heart of joint delivery arrangements is designing and/or improving services so that service users get a better experience and stronger outcomes. For it to work the following things need to happen.

Senior management must be committed to it

Trustees and senior staff must be able and willing to demonstrate their commitment to joint delivery. This may involve their being willing to overcome any traditional rivalries that have existed between organisations.

It must be given a fresh look

To design joined-up services organisations must look at them from the user's perspective rather than from the perspective of the professionals who design and manage services. This can mean that you need to look at an individual service as a part of a bigger system and evaluate how different users move between and experience services.

It must be given some resources

To support joint delivery, organisations may need to contribute some resources to pay for changes in technology, staff training and other activities. The biggest resource is probably staff time spent on developing joint delivery mechanisms.

There needs to be a willingness to work differently

Effective joint delivery does require all staff to see things from a wider perspective. This can challenge the traditional ways in which people are trained and also how job roles are designed.

There must be fast communication systems when things go wrong

Organisations which sign up to joint delivery need to have reliable and quick communication systems so that they can inform each other of problems, track progress and identify and resolve obstacles. Having up-to-date technology should aid this issue.

As joint delivery develops, it is often useful to record what has been agreed and ensure that any new joint-delivery process is fully supported by the organisation and is built into relevant management processes.

Shared services

Sharing services is a simple and logical idea. Organisations stay independent, but agree that some specific activities should be jointly delivered across organisations. Examples include:

- Organisations pooling resources to operate from a single building with a single access point.
- Organisations sharing back-office administrative services such as bookkeeping, IT support and personnel management.

In the public sector, shared services are currently high on the agenda, as local authorities and other public sector agencies experiment with sharing services such as computer services, facilities management and professional support across organisations. Some experiments have included having one chief executive working across two neighbouring local authorities.

A range of factors usually motivates the sharing of services:

- **Cost saving:** sharing services is often seen as a way of being a leaner organisation and cutting out duplication.
- **Best use of resources:** shared services could mean that a service is fully used.
- **Added value:** sharing something which would not be available to organisations on their own. Organisations that might not be able to justify or afford having a service for their own use can access a service through collaborative venture.

The manager of a local social care charity described her experience:

> As our organisation grew we needed to build up our administration systems. We got to a stage where we needed good and reliable computer support, but we could not afford to employ an IT support worker. In conversations with other local voluntary sector managers I realised that we were not alone in this. The idea emerged that our three organisations could afford to pool our resources and jointly employ a worker. We have done this and it seems to be working well. One

organisation has the role as the worker's line manager and the three of us meet together to review and plan the service. It means we can have someone who understands our systems and is part of our team, but not on a full-time basis. I am interested in how sharing services could develop. We could look at using this model in other areas such as financial management and for things like bid writing.

How shared services work

Usually one of the organisations involved acts as the lead or managing body. It has the responsibility for employing and supervising shared staff, for administrating the service and for collecting fees from the other partners. The partners in the venture should agree and document the following things:

Levels of services

Exactly what services are to be shared? What level of service delivery should partners be able to expect? Shared services can attract VAT, so organisations should take appropriate advice.

Payment rates

How much will partners be expected to pay for the services? Can partners buy extra services if there is capacity and, if so, at what price?

Line management arrangements

Who will employ and manage staff who are involved in shared services? How will support and supervision be given? How will problems be resolved?

For a shared service to work, we would suggest that the following four factors are taken into account:

1. Accountability and flexibility

Staff who work across organisations need to know to whom they are accountable and how to obtain support. They must be flexible enough to be able to organise their time and work in different locations with different styles and working cultures.

2. A focus on outcomes/no micro-management

Using a shared service can involve managers having less direct day-to-day control over an activity. Some shared services have collapsed because managers have been inclined to meddle and over-control them. To avoid this, managers must focus on ensuring that the shared services outcome is what they want and be willing to leave people to get on with it.

3. Fairness

Partners need to ensure that everyone is getting a fair use of the shared service. There needs to be regular monitoring of the service's performance to check that all partners are getting a fair share.

4. Regular reviews

It is useful if the partners review the shared service periodically to check that it is delivering what partners need and want. This can help to update and renew services.

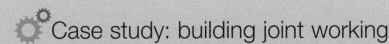

Case study: building joint working

Through regular informal contact three organisations, Leeds Advocacy, Advocacy Support and Advocacy for Mental Health and Dementia identified that there was a logical case for greater cooperation and a more formal approach to collaboration.

In a series of facilitated workshops the three organisations' managers and trustees identified several areas where working together could lead to potential gains. Possible advantages included:

Service delivery
- Create a single point of access
- Share relief workers
- Improve the reach of the service
- Set up specialist services

Organisational management
- Offer joint training
- Share monitoring
- Do joint contract bidding
- Procedure development
- Organise shared IT support

Strategic development
- Combine publicity costs
- Bid for new work
- Plan future strategy

All of this was in the context of a tough commissioning round and likely pressure from commissioners to demonstrate that the organisations could provide a full and comprehensive service to all potential clients.

Through discussions, the managers considered a range of options and structures that could develop joint working and also how best to use a network organisation called Advonet, which had previously been created to provide shared services.

Throughout the process, the discussion focused on how collaboration could increase the level of quality advocacy and how any structure would add value to the business of service delivery.

At the end of the process it was agreed to transform Advonet into a joint bidding mechanism run by the organisations, with a brief to win contracts on behalf of the member organisations.

On reflecting on the process three factors were found to be important:

1. The need to focus on developing and improving the ability of the three organisations to work to their shared mission. To collaborate successfully, they needed a positive and realistic vision of what could be achieved by working together.

2. The need to get discussions to go beyond the three managers. Trustees, staff and volunteers had to be kept informed and involved. It was also essential to talk with key funders to ensure that they understood what was being proposed so that they could, at best, confirm their support or, at least, see no problems with it.

3. The need to get organisations to commit and agree to things formally. It was important to firm up people's verbal commitment by moving to a more formal agreement.

Making it formal

All of these joint arrangements need to have some sort of written agreement that sets out the intention of the arrangement and how it should operate. Putting together the arrangement needs careful consideration and a willingness to see ahead and identify potential problems or even conflicts.

A member of a children's services partnership commented on her experience of putting an agreement together:

> Four years ago, when we first started meeting together everything was quite informal and friendly. All of the main players knew and trusted each other. We put off discussions about agreements and potential problems. Eventually we did come up with an agreement. I am very glad that we did. Over the past years we have had to deal with new people joining and a simmering disagreement between two members. Having the agreement gave us a structure to discuss things and also a process to resolve problems. I have learnt that when everything is going well you still have to think about what might happen when things change.

Joint agreements

A joint agreement needs to cover the following headings:

Who the arrangement is between
Who are the parties to the agreement?

The purpose of the agreement
What is the overall intention? What do the parties commit to in terms of service quality and ethos?

The scope of the agreement
What activities does the agreement cover?

What each party commits to do
Describe in specific terms what each party will do.

Decisions and organisational process
How will the collaboration be organised? Where and how will decisions be made? What will be expected of the parties?

Information
What information will be collated to monitor performance?

Resource management
How will the budget be drawn up and managed? How will management and overhead costs be allocated?

Dispute resolution
How will disagreements or problems between parties be resolved? Give options for mediation and arbitration.

End of agreement
What will happen at the end of the agreement? Who will own any resources or intellectual capital?

Making joint working work

In reality, written agreements can help the process, but are not guarantees that parties will cooperate and work for a mutual gain. The following ten pointers have been found to help different joint ventures be effective:

1. Have a clear focus

Joint arrangements need a sense of purpose. All parties must understand what difference they are trying to make and what gap they are trying to fill. A useful exercise is to discuss and agree what success would look like in two to three years' time. Without a clear focus, joint ventures can degenerate into talking shops.

2. Create sound management arrangements

To avoid confusion the management arrangements for joint arrangements need to be transparent and unambiguous. Staff working on a joint project need to know to whom they are accountable. Responsibilities for tasks need to be clearly delegated and recorded.

3. Allow difference

Working in partnership with another organisation does not mean that you have to give up on your identity, style and culture. Effective partnerships allow and respect differences between parties.

4. Establish good and fast monitoring systems

Good measurement and monitoring systems should be established to report on progress and flag up any problems or setbacks in performance. Managers will need to make time to study performance data and be willing to act on it.

5. Maintain accurate systems for costing and allocating resources

Joint-working arrangements need to have accurate systems to fully cost any activities that the organisations are involved in. Such costing needs to take into account the full cost of the activity, including the cost of managing it. Full costing is particularly important to ensure that parties do not inadvertently have to subsidise a joint venture.

6. Allow time to build the partnership

Time needs to be set aside to enable parties to develop a style of working and to build up effective working practices between parties.

7. Create a shared view of quality

For a joint venture to work, all of the parties involved in managing it need to have a similar view of what constitutes good practice and what users or communities should be able to expect. One approach is to develop a quality framework setting out basic and clear standards that should be applied consistently across all activities.

8. Have regular reviews

Time needs to be built in for all parties to review how the partnership has developed and identify any obstacles in the way of progress. Discussions should focus on the following questions:

- Is a joint arrangement still relevant and needed?
- What works?
- What needs attention?
- How might the arrangement develop?

9. Schedule regular report-back dates

There should be regular and structured appointments for designated people to report back to all of the parties on how the joint arrangement is operating. Such appointments should remind people of the intention behind collaborating and help people who are new to it to understand it.

10. Watch out for 'mission creep'

There is a danger that a joint arrangement might start to expand its operations and begin pursuing work and funding opportunities which are beyond its original remit. This can create major problems. Decisions to move into new areas need to be taken strategically and should involve all the partners.

Chapter five
Lead-partner and subcontracting models

This chapter explores different ways in which organisations can move to more formal ways of collaborating and delivering. It will focus on two approaches:

1. a lead-partner model;
2. subcontracting between organisations.

Both these models are designed to enable organisations to divide up an activity and have a clear process for delivering it.

A lead-partner model usually operates by one organisation being appointed by the others to take responsibility for managing the contract. The work is then divided up amongst the other parties.

A subcontractor model occurs when one organisation comes to an agreement with another organisation that they will be paid to deliver an element of the contract or provide a service.

The distinction can be described as follows.

Lead-partner model

- The lead partner is appointed by the partners.
- The lead partner is accountable to the partners.
- Decisions are made by consensus.

Subcontracting model

- The main contractor selects the subcontractors.
- The subcontractors are accountable to the main contractor.
- The main contractor is in a business relationship with the sub-contractors.

Examples of lead-partner and subcontracting models

1. A complex supply chain arrangement in the delivery of government work contracts whereby a commissioner appoints a limited number of contractors (known as 'prime contractors') to deliver programmes in an area. The prime contractors then appoint other agencies to do some or all of the direct service delivery.

2. Some organisations come together to bid for and deliver major contracts. One party takes on the legal responsibility for the contract and is accountable to the funder for its performance. The lead body coordinates and manages the work of the other parties.

3. An organisation brings in an organisation with specialist skills or knowledge to deliver aspects of a contract rather than set up a specialist or in-house unit.

The following sections explain the models in more detail.

Lead-partner model

This model is a way of organisations coming together to share the delivery of a project, but allows the commissioner to contract with a single organisation which is then accountable for the delivery of the whole contract to time, budget and quality standards.

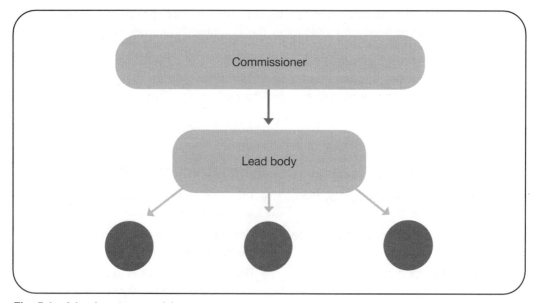

Fig. 5.1 A lead-partner model.

As illustrated in figure 5.1, the lead body acts on behalf of the other members, but at the same time the lead body is accountable to the commissioner for the proper and efficient delivery of the contract. The lead body has to have the capacity to manage and organise the project properly and must have the resources to monitor the other partner's or partners' performance.

It is important to make a distinction between a lead-partner arrangement and a subcontracting one. Although they are similar in parts there is a different style and set of power relationships. In some cases tensions and problems occur because the precise nature of relationships between parties has not been clarified or worked through. In a few cases, the motivation of lead partners for inviting others to work with them may not be for the best of reasons, as one of the following case studies will show.

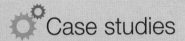 Case studies

Just a delivery mechanism

A trustee of a neighbourhood centre described her experience:

We were very pleased to be asked by a national charity to work with them. Their Area Manager said all the right things about shared values, common goals and all working together. We felt that by working with them we could be part of a much bigger programme. A year down the line I wish we had probed it a bit further. They see us as part of their 'delivery mechanism'. All the emphasis is on meeting targets, controlling cost and getting people through the door. We are losing our ability to control the services we run.

Bid candy

At first, the trustees of the Mangrove Centre had been flattered to be invited to be part of a bid to win a government regeneration programme led by Progress, a large national social enterprise.

Bid meetings were tightly managed by the Progress's Business Development Manager. At best the Mangrove Centre was expected to 'nod things through and sign up for it'. The Mangrove Centre's Coordinator expressed serious concerns about the process.

It became really obvious that we were invited to give their bid some local credibility, as we are a well-established centre that reflects the diversity of our community. We have local knowledge, credibility and contacts. We were being used as 'bid candy' to make them look good. We were very much the junior partner in the bid. We had little access to the bid costings and details of the bid.

Next time someone invites us to be part of a partnership, I intend to ask lots of questions and do a lot of challenging to find out why we are really being invited in. We need to start valuing more what we bring to partnerships.

Why use a lead-partner model?

There are several reasons why organisations have adopted a lead-partner model.

- It stops organisations having to bid against each other and duplicate effort.
- It can allow smaller or developing organisations that may not have the organisational capacity or experience to win a bid on their own to be part of a programme.
- It builds on existing strong relationships between parties.
- Sometimes commissioners encourage it, as it means that they only have to work with a limited number of providers.

Role definition

The way the role of lead partner gets played out varies considerably. In some instances it is simply an administrative one, whereas in others the lead partner has considerable influence and control.

What does the lead partner do?

Typical roles played by lead bodies in collaborative arrangements are as follows.

Role	Possible tasks involved
Bidding for the contract	Drawing up and submitting the bid on behalf of and in consultation with the other partners.
Holding the contract	Being the named accountable body; i.e. having full legal responsibility for the proper delivery of the contract/agreement with funders.
External point of contact	Acting as the public contact point for the partnership.
Secretariat	Organising and hosting partnership meetings. Following up decisions. Maintaining records.
Monitoring performance	Obtaining regular performance measures and reports from partners. Collating, verifying and reporting to the commissioner on performance.
Contract management	Claiming monies. Holding contract resources. Paying partners.
Communications	Running internal communications. Conducting a media role. Producing a partnership bulletin and website.
Performance management	Progress-chasing. Problem-solving.

All of the partners involved should discuss and agree the ways in which these roles should be carried out. The lead partner should be able to work out how much of its own organisation's time and resources will need to be allocated to being the lead partner. The cost of the lead-partner role is usually included in any project costing as a management or overhead charge. Often the lead body will incur considerable costs from writing and submitting a funding bid on behalf of all of the parties.

To be the lead partner you need certain key skills and expertise. From studying various arrangements we would suggest that effective lead partners need the following skills:

1. **Group leadership and facilitation skills**. Lead partners should have the ability to help people from partner agencies feel part of something. They need to have the

skills to run effective meetings, encourage communication and develop a common purpose between partners.

2. **Sound organisational skills.** The lead partner needs systems and skills to ensure that partnership decisions get implemented, work gets followed through, deadlines are met and progress is chased.

3. **Strong business management skills.** Lead partners need to fully understand how their business works. They need to know any contract and funding agreement inside out and also be able to negotiate and work with funders and commissioners.

Getting it right

The following pointers are designed to help the lead-partner role to develop:

1. **Role clarity.** All parties need to understand what the role of the lead party is and what is expected of all other parties. It is useful to set this out in some sort of partnership agreement or terms of reference.

2. **Financial transparency.** There needs to be agreement on what financial information the lead partner needs to produce to show how the programme is operating and the real costs involved.

3. **Time for the role.** The lead partner cannot simply add on the role to other tasks and duties carried out in its organisation. It must allocate time for carrying out the work involved in being lead partner.

4. **Addition of value.** It is useful to check periodically that the arrangement is still meeting its original objectives. Does it enable partners to do things together that they would not be able to do on their own? Is there a danger of the lead-partner arrangement degenerating into just another layer of management?

5. **Openness about risk.** The lead partner needs to feel comfortable about taking on an extra level of organisational risk. Potential scenarios need to be talked through. For example, if one partner failed to deliver or did something which caused a major contract breach, would the lead partner, as the accountable body, feel comfortable about being held responsible for it?

6. **Clear delegation.** The lead-partner organisation must be able to delegate to partners. It must be willing to manage at a distance and accept that it cannot direct or control every aspect of what each partner does.

7. **Personal relationships.** The staff working in the lead-partner role must be willing to build up credible and effective working relationships with partners. This will involve their providing support to partners and helping them with systems and processes.

8. **Early-warning systems.** The lead partner needs monitoring systems that quickly identify problems and enable it to respond.

9. **Time for strategy and planning ahead.** Much of the lead partner's work is organisational: processing finance, keeping records and ensuring that things happen. The lead partner needs to make time to think and plan ahead. It needs to be tuned into trends and developments and able to spot potential opportunities.

It can take some time to get the relationships right. The coordinator of a community group that acted as lead body for a regeneration initiative described how it worked from the lead-body's perspective:

> It has taken us two years to work out how to play the lead-body role. At one level we had to pick up all the things that other people didn't want to do: compiling reports, data management, bid writing and chasing payment.

> Playing the intermediary between the funder and the groups was also tricky – it felt at times that we were being pulled in the middle. Also, trustees grew concerned that we could be legally responsible for the failure of one of the parties to deliver.

Over time, it has got better. We have firmed up the relationship and made it clear that groups have to cooperate with us. We have also had to remind some groups that they would not have got the funding on their own as they did not have the admin systems and management capacity to bid for and manage such a large programme on their own. Most people now see the partnership as something that works in their interest and adds real value.

Case study: Manchester's One Stop Advice Project – an exercise in collaboration

In 2008, Manchester City Council commissioned a major review of advice services in the city. The review found that while the quality of advice was generally high, the way provision was organised lacked integration and was fragmented. The review described how clients were bumped around the system and sometimes gave up on their quest for advice. It was also clear that funders and commissioners, in particular the Legal Services Commission, were frustrated by the number of advice providers in Manchester and the lack of any coordinated service.

An alliance of advice agencies, The Manchester Community Legal Advice Services Partnership, grasped this challenge and successfully applied to the Big Lottery for funding to develop a One Stop Advice Project led by Manchester Citizens Advice Bureau.

So far the project has:

- designed and set up a virtual call centre;
- established an online appointment, booking and referral service covering the whole city;
- launched a website;
- developed touch-screen information kiosks;
- designed and launched a smartphone information app.

The project to date has helped 37,611 clients and a further 17,000 per annum have appointments made using the system. It has maintained a partnership involving over 20 different and varied advice providers.

Prue Yeoman, the programme manager, identified four factors as being key in making the project a success:

1. *Top management commitment. A critical factor in the project's success was getting and maintaining 'buy-in' from managers in each of the partner organisations. They have to see the collaboration as useful and fitting with their own direction.*
2. *Focus on the client. The starting point has to be the ability to demonstrate how the project would make a real and tangible difference to clients. The project needed to demonstrate how it would improve people's access to advice services practically.*
3. *Emphasis on delivery. The project team needed to be skilled in project management and delivery. It was critical to move from talking about it to doing it.*
4. *Keep building and rebuilding the partnership. Many of the organisations that make up the partnership have little history of collaborating with each other. The lead body and the project team has had to work hard to promote a shared vision of what was possible and develop a style of working that was open and respected the different ways of operating amongst partners.*

When it goes wrong

There may come a time in the life of an arrangement where some or all players start to feel that it is not working or is not productive. The partnership agreement or terms of reference should give guidance on how to change or dissolve the arrangement; however, before such action is taken, you should consider whether the lead-body arrangement could evolve into a more formal subcontracting one.

In one educational partnership, the lead-partner organisation withdrew as it did not feel comfortable with the level of risk and felt that its reputation was dependent on the performance of others. The lead-partner model was replaced by a subcontracting one that gave the lead partner greater control and more of a supervisory capacity.

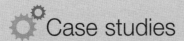 Case studies

The lead body: stuck in the middle

With the support of their local authority, six voluntary organisations had come together under the umbrella of a voluntary sector infrastructure organisation to bid for and deliver a contract providing home care support to adult social care clients.

Putting the bid together proved to be a major task, as each organisation had different approaches, policies and practices. After much discussion and negotiation, a successful bid was tendered by the infrastructure organisation that agreed to take on the contract, be the lead body and subcontract the work out to the six consortium members.

The Director of the infrastructure organisation reflected on his experience:

With hindsight, it's obvious we were bounced into it. We relied too much on personal links and promises of cooperation. Although we delivered the contract, at times it was touch and go! Three things proved difficult:

1. *We lacked a proper mechanism for dividing the contract delivery up.*
2. *Although we called it a subcontracting arrangement we never really thought about what would happen if one of the six organisations failed to deliver. We did not have a proper and quick mechanism for intervening or applying sanctions. One organisation's failure could have damaged the whole contract.*
3. *Our role as the lead body was an awkward and demanding one. The local authority kept urgently demanding more and more information and naturally dealt with us rather than the providers. We then had to keep pestering the organisations for data and information. They just wanted to be left to get on with the face-to-face work. At times it felt that we had all the responsibility without the authority.*

We have now embarked on a process of firming up the arrangement in preparation for the contract's re-tender. We have developed a very clear agreement with partners, setting out expectations and responsibilities. As the lead body, we are going to have to be much clearer and tougher.

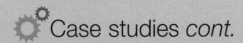 Case studies *cont.*

A small fish

A manager of a youth project recounted some pitfalls she encountered when working with a lead partner:

> We were invited to be part of a joint bid and at first it seemed a positive and logical thing to do. We were attracted to the idea of 'strength in numbers' and thought that bidding and working together could deliver up some real gains.
>
> A local housing association assumed the role of lead partner. They were never really appointed to it. This was a big mistake as they obviously saw it as 'their contract' and that community groups like ours were 'bit players there to add local colour and make up the numbers'.
>
> Problems soon developed. The lead body acted in quite secretive ways. They creamed off the most interesting and lucrative bits of the contract. They also took quite a generous management fee in payment for their role as lead body. I have learnt a lot from the process. A lead body must be accountable and committed to working with the other partners.

Subcontracting model

A subcontracting relationship is a simple one. The organisation that holds the contract makes a business relationship with another body to deliver all or part of that organisation's work on its behalf.

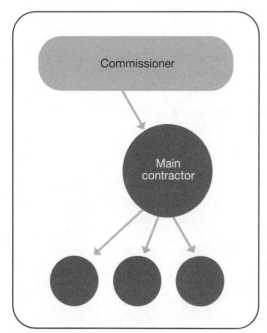

Fig. 5.2 A subcontracting model.

This model is based on a typical business or commercial arrangement. Subcontracting might be an option when the organisation that holds the contract needs to:

- bring in extra capacity to deliver a service;
- bring in a specialist agency with a particular expertise or skill;
- expand, but prefers to outsource rather than increase the size of its own organisation.

Subcontracting or outsourcing is increasingly common in the private sector as companies use external providers to meet demand and retain some flexibility. Early examples of subcontracting in the voluntary sector usually concerned organisations which lacked the resources in-house using third parties to deliver an element of a programme.

One of the biggest examples of subcontracting has been the delivery of the government's welfare to work programme. The Department of Work and Pensions selected prime contractors to deliver Work Programme contracts in England and Wales. Each prime contractor then appointed local providers on a subcontractor basis. The conditions and nature of the contracts have caused some controversy, as some subcontractors have struggled to make them viable. In some instances, subcontractors did not get the level of work from their prime contractor necessary to make the contract viable (Ainsworth 2012). Other subcontractors have complained that the contracts have been very inflexible and have tried to restrict the ability of voluntary organisations to campaign or intervene in policy debates.

As more public services move out to tender, some organisations have come together to bid with one clear main contractor and with others acting as subcontractors in the bid. Subcontractors can play a key role in using their specific expertise and knowledge to develop and shape the bid.

Types of subcontracting

Subcontracting happens in different formats. Here are four types:

Type	Description	Example
1. Outsourcing a complete function or activity	Rather than having a particular function or activity provided by directly employed in-house staff, the delivery of the service is contracted out to a third party.	A voluntary organisation that had grown rapidly contracted out various functions such as managing its minibus fleet and the design and operation of its website to other voluntary organisations with particular skills and expertise.
2. Subcontracting part of a project or contract delivery	An element of a project or contract is subcontracted to another agency to deliver.	A community development agency appointed a local community group to deliver education classes, as the group had contacts within the community that the agency lacked.
3. Buying in a specialist expertise or skill	An organisation hires another organisation to bring in a particular skill or expertise that it lacks.	A social care agency appointed an advice agency to deliver a series of benefit checks and money advice sessions to its clients.
4. Having a back-up or on-call facility	An arrangement is made whereby an organisation can call on another service to provide support when demand is high.	A housing charity negotiated a service agreement with a similar agency to use its support staff if the charity had a particular peak in demand.

Pros and cons of subcontracting
From the main contractor's position

Pros

- Able to be flexible and react quickly to cope with peaks and troughs in demand.
- Does not have to get involved in the detail of the service management – can focus on outcomes.
- Easier to control costs – only pay the subcontractor for the services delivered.
- Can be a way of bringing in expertise and specialist skills without having to manage and grow them in-house.

Cons

- Danger of being too dependent on the subcontractor.
- Risk of the subcontractor not delivering.
- Can be difficult to ensure that the subcontractor and its staff work to and are committed to the contractor's standards, ethos and values.
- Can be expensive.
- Risk of the commissioner feeling it loses control because the service is being partly delivered by a subcontractor.

From the subcontractor's position

Pros

- Might be able to get a share of bigger contracts and services.
- Able to develop a particular expertise and specialist functions.
- A way to ensure that all of the organisation's resources are fully used.
- Can provide a valuable form of income especially for niche or specialist functions.

Cons

- Concern that subcontractors get offered the worst aspects of the contract.
- Danger of the main contractor micro-managing delivery or over-interfering.
- Staff having to work in a different culture.
- Danger of insecurity: contracts could be easily withdrawn or reduced.

In reviewing subcontracting relationships, the following key issues emerged.

1. The reasons for subcontracting

It is important to be clear as to the intentions behind subcontracting. Is it to cover a temporary rise in demand? Is it to buy in a particular expertise or specialism? Is it intended to be a long-term relationship or to fill a short-term need? Answers to these questions will shape the nature of the subcontracting relationship.

2. Risk transfer

Subcontracting involves putting responsibilities for delivery onto another party. It involves transferring, but not losing, ultimate risk and responsibility. Blaming a project's failure to deliver on the inadequacies of a subcontractor is not an acceptable defence. It is important that the risk element in a subcontracting relationship is properly analysed and discussed. Could the failure of a subcontractor damage your standing and reputation? Are you comfortable to assume that a third party will manage and deliver an activity in your name?

⚙ Case study: managing subcontracting

The manager of the Dover Street Community Arts Centre described her organisation as 'the ultimate virtual organisation – scratch the surface and the centre is little more than a collection of subcontracting relationships'.

Due to funding uncertainties we employ hardly anyone on a permanent basis, so when we get funding or contracts to deliver programmes we will usually subcontract out a lot of the delivery to organisations and groups that we feel confident in working with. They do the work in our name. We oversee it and ensure that it is done to the agreed standard. Last year we won a bid with the local authority to run a week-long community festival. Much of the delivery was contracted out to local groups; the festival website, the schools programme and a sports event were all delivered by local projects operating under our brand. It worked well as it used their skills and contacts and meant we did not have to move into areas outside of our skill set.

For it to work we had to make it very clear that it was a contractual relationship about delivery and not some vague or fuzzy partnership. We have to be confident that they will perform and do it properly – blaming failure to deliver on a subcontractor is no defence when things go wrong.

Getting the working relationship right with subcontractors (or 'delivery partners', as we sometimes call them) is crucial. Our job is to coordinate all of the different activities and make sure that they see how their work fits into a bigger picture. Also it is important that once the arrangement has been set up we let the subcontractor get on with it. As the main contractor we have to be good at delegating and focus on the outcomes and try not to meddle.

3. You need to know what you are managing

A key danger in a subcontracting relationship is becoming too dependent on the subcontractor. The main party who appoints the subcontractor needs to retain some control and an awareness of what is being subcontracted. The director of a charity described his experience of subcontracting the development and maintenance of the charity's website:

The organisation we subcontracted it to was very strong on technical expertise. This worked well until we started experiencing problems. We were totally reliant on them to fix it. We lacked the knowledge and technical capacity to direct and evaluate their work. We were totally reliant on what they told us. Just because you have subcontracted or outsourced something doesn't mean that you have to give up on it. For the relationship to work you have to retain a level of understanding and competence to avoid being entirely dependent on the subcontractor.

Effective subcontracting

⚙ Case study: Craigville Advice Services and Daisyhill Venture Centre

The award of a major contract to Craigville Advice Services represented a major step forward. A key part of the contract was to develop and run a financial awareness campaign on the Daisyhill estate – an isolated post-war estate on the edge of Craigville. The estate had a reputation as being very difficult to work on and there was some resistance to organisations 'suddenly parachuting into the area – offering loads of things and then disappearing', as one local councillor described it.

The Coordinator of Craigville Advice Services approached the Manager of the Daisyhill Venture Centre to discuss possibilities of working together. After a few meetings they agreed an arrangement whereby the advice agency would subcontract the delivery of the financial awareness campaign to the centre. They agreed the following role split:

Craigville Advice Services

- Pay the centre an agreed fee covering all direct project costs and a contribution to overheads.
- Provide training, resources and casework supervision to the project worker.
- Work with the project to ensure that agreed standards are in place.
- Take part in a project steering group.
- Carry out a six-month and mid-point project evaluation.
- Manage relationships with the project's funder.
- Involve the project worker in campaign team meetings.
- Develop a future project plan to carry the work on.

Daisyhill Venture Centre

- Employ and supervise a part-time project worker.
- Provide office space and resources for the project worker.
- Ensure that the project operates to agreed standards.
- Set up and run a steering group to support the project.
- Promote and market the service in Daisyhill.
- Produce monitoring and other reports as required.
- Take part in future project planning.

The role description formed a major part of the service-level agreement between the organisations.

It worked!

At the project mid-point review, both parties described the subcontracting relationship as a successful one.

The Manager of the Daisyhill Venture Centre described it as follows:

> The arrangement enabled us to get a worker onto the estate that we would not have been able to get on our own. We were too small and lacked the technical expertise in money management and debt issues, and back-up systems to win the contract on our own. The worker is part of our team, but can draw down support and help from the main organisation.

The Coordinator of Craigville Advice Services commented:

> Subcontracting the project to the lead community organisation on the estate has worked. The worker has been able to use the centre's networks, contacts and communication channels to get the project started. Without that progress, it would have been much slower.

Both managers commented that having a clear agreement gave a sense of discipline to the arrangement:

> We know what is expected of each other. The arrangement has played to our strengths: Craigville has the credibility and expertise to win the contract and provide technical support and external supervision to the project. The centre has the profile, contacts and standing in the community to make it work. It is a win-win arrangement.

Subcontracting 'what ifs . . . '

A useful way of testing out how a subcontracting arrangement will work is to develop and play out some possible scenarios of what could happen during a subcontracting arrangement. Such scenarios should test how useful the formal agreement between parties would be in resolving problems and also help to clarify and build the nature and style of the relationship between the parties.

Here are five scenarios that could occur in a subcontracting relationship (hopefully not all at the same time!)

1. The expected work does not materialise

What happens if the work expected from the main contractor does not turn up? A health charity was appointed by another charity as a subcontractor to provide a specialist counselling service. The main contractor was confident that it would have a steady stream of clients needing the specialist service and agreed a contract whereby the specialist would get paid a unit fee for each client referred. A mixture of reasons, including administrative failings, poor publicity and communication difficulties, meant that in the first few months of the agreement the charity received very few referrals and consequently little income. What level of guarantee or protection does the subcontractor need?

2. The subcontractor wants to deliver the service in a different way

Is there a danger of the main contractor over-directing how the service should be delivered and organised? What flexibility does the agreement give to the subcontractor to respond to user or community needs or develop services that in its view best meet needs? Could a subcontracting agreement reduce flexibility and responsiveness? If a subcontractor found a better way of delivering the contract outcomes that was supported by the users, would the agreement let it run the service in that way or would it have to do it in the way prescribed by the main contractor?

3. A service user has a serious grievance

If a service user has a serious complaint or grievance, against whom should they take action? Should it be against the main contractor which the user might have had first contact with or should it be against the subcontractor that the main contractor referred the client to? Who gets sued? Can the subcontractor indemnify the main contractor against the risk of action?

4. Costs rise steeply

How will the arrangement manage exceptional rises in costs that could not have been predicted at the start of the agreement? If essential costs such as fuel prices rise during the period of the contract, does the subcontractor have to accommodate them?

5. What happens at the end?

Who is responsible for managing the closure and any post-contract work or liabilities? Who owns any equipment or materials developed during the contract?

These issues and similar 'what ifs...' should be worked through by both parties so that there is clarity about the nature of the relationship. The subcontracting agreement should provide a structure to the relationship and a process for resolving any differences or disagreements.

Outline content of a subcontracting agreement

Subcontracting agreements vary considerably in terms of detail, content and structure. A good subcontracting agreement should set out the nature of the arrangement between the parties, what each party is expected to do, the financial arrangements and also how disputes and problems should be resolved. Full and proper legal advice should be sought in drawing up a contract, but the following list outlines the key points.

Who the contract is between	Who are the parties to the contract? Main contractor and subcontractor.
Overall purpose of the contract	What is the overall intention of the contract? For example, 'to deliver a high-quality training programme for unemployed people in Anytown'. What values or principles should underpin the delivery and management of the arrangement?
Duration of the contract	How long is the contract for? Fixed term: ends on a set date. Rolling agreement: for a set period, but can be continued if both parties agree.
What the main contractor will be expected to do	What will the main contractor be expected to do, organise and arrange to enable the contract to operate?
What the subcontractor will be expected to do	What services will the subcontractor be expected to deliver?
Service arrangements	What service standards or minimum practice levels will the subcontractor be expected to adhere to?
Monitoring arrangements	How will contract performance be managed? What data and key performance indicators will the subcontractor need to collate? How will performance data be analysed and used?

Management arrangements	How will arrangements regarding specific issues be made? For example, regarding: ● publicity and communications; ● specific policies and procedures; ● ownership of materials; ● what happens at the end of the contract.
Complaints procedure	How will any complaints be managed? How and when will the main contractor be involved in complaints?
Financial arrangements	How much will the subcontractor be paid for the contract? Payment dates. Any circumstances where the payment may be altered or varied, such as if performance is poor or if particular costs increase.
Disputes	The procedure for resolving disagreements between parties.
Contact points	Who are the relevant contact points in both parties for managing the contract?
Variation	The process for negotiating changes to the contract.
Termination	Are there any circumstances where either party could end the contract?
Agreement	Formal signed agreement

Chapter six
Consortia and joint ventures

A consortium is an organisation of two or more bodies which have chosen to create a separate structure in order to pool their activities to achieve a shared goal.

This chapter will look at two types of consortium working:

1. **Bidding consortia** where a new body is established to bid for and share out contracts to its member organisations.
2. **Joint ventures** where organisations stay independent but create a new venture to deliver a shared function.

Bidding consortia

Over the past few years, organisations have joined together to create consortia in increasing numbers to bid for and manage the delivery of large contracts. A consortium is a specially created membership body that can perform a number of functions. It can:

- submit bids as a consortium and then share the work out amongst members on a subcontracting basis;
- act as the one point of contact between commissioners and voluntary and community organisations;
- research and circulate information about contracting opportunities amongst its members;
- encourage members to share information and collaborate;
- help to develop member organisations' skills and capacity to deliver contracts and deliver good services through training, support and sharing best practice.

Consortia usually adopt the model shown in figure 6.1.

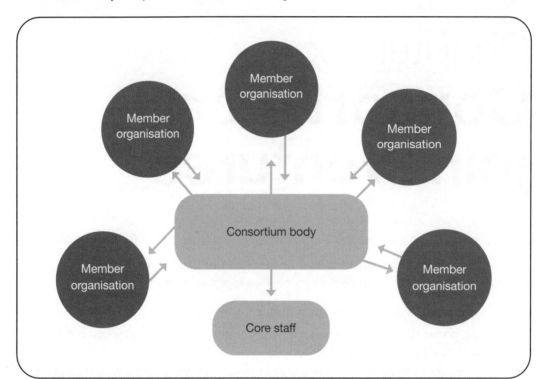

Fig. 6.1 A bidding consortium model.

The model, often referred to as a 'hub and spoke' organisation, has the following features. Member organisations usually have to apply to be in membership. In most instances, they have to demonstrate that they have and practise clear policies and procedures and are able to operate and deliver services to a consistent standard. A consortium needs to develop and agree some criteria for membership and a way of checking that applicants and existing members meet agreed standards. This process can give a consortium an advantage in bidding for contracts, as it can show that all parties to the bid have met a quality threshold.

The consortium is usually constituted as an independent organisation so that, as an independently constituted body, it can bid for and manage contracts in its own right.

When and if the consortium wins contracts, the delivery of the contract is shared out amongst member organisations. The consortium needs to have a subcontracting agreement with members to govern this relationship. It retains an agreed portion of the contract as a management fee to cover its central management and organisation costs. The consortium is accountable to the commissioners for the proper delivery of the contract. It will be responsible for liaising with the commissioner and ensuring that all monitoring and performance data is properly collected.

To carry out these tasks, the consortium needs some kind of staff team. The staff team might be direct employees of the consortium or in some cases are staff seconded from another organisation (such as a Council for Voluntary Service) or from a member organisation. The consortium's core staff can usually play the following roles:

- **Consortium management:** administrating and running the consortium as an organisation; servicing and supporting the board and acting as the first point of contact.
- **Business development:** building links with commissioners, spotting potential business opportunities and marketing the sector as a competent provider.
- **Bid writing:** completing pre-qualification questionnaires, submitting bids and leading the bid development process.
- **Capacity building:** helping members improve their practice and ensure that they are ready to deliver contracts.
- **Contract management:** liaising with commissioners, ensuring that all monitoring and contract management processes are completed.
- **Delivery support:** supporting partners in delivery, firefighting any problems and encouraging collaboration between members.

Thought should be given as to how the consortium will itself be funded. Most existing ones have developed a business model in which the consortium generates income from the following sources:

- membership fees from consortium members;
- start-up grants and loans;
- management fees from all contracts won: 'top slicing';
- charging members for additional services such as training and management support.

To be financially viable, the consortium must win a minimum level of contract business to break even and pay for its central functions.

A key challenge that faces a new consortium is not having a track record or any evidence of past work as an independent organisation in its own right. Commissioners may need to be persuaded that the track record of the organisations that make up the consortium meet this requirement.

Several consortia have been successful in winning start-up funding, either as a grant or as a loan, from agencies such as the Social Investment Business Group.

Consortia and commissioners

In developing a consortium it is useful to approach potential commissioners to ensure that they understand the model and method of working. A consortium can be an attractive offer for commissioners, as it can:

- offer a single point of contact;
- make communication between a range of parties easier and encourage the providers which are members of the consortium to work together;
- overcome traditional boundaries; and
- produce better services and better value by combining experience.

However, often there is a need to overcome some of the concerns and anxieties that commissioners and, in particular, procurement managers might have about consortia working. One long-serving local authority contracts manager expressed his concerns:

> *Although I can see the advantages in organisations working together to deliver services, I need to know that the lines of accountability and responsibility are clear. If something goes wrong or performance fails, we need to know who to deal with and who is ultimately responsible. Joint arrangements must have clear and simple structures. A consortium needs to be more than a paper organisation. It needs to have systems and processes in place to act fast.*

In developing a consortium that is intended to bid for contracts, attention should be given to the following points:

- To whom will the contracts be awarded? Will the contracts be held by the consortium in its own right?
- What sort of subcontracting arrangement will be needed between the consortium and its members?
- How will the consortium divide up the work? Will members have to bid to the consortium for a share of any contract?
- Will the consortium have to have its own quality-assurance systems, policies and procedures in order to bid successfully or will it be able to rely upon those of member organisations to meet the requirements of any pre-qualification questionnaire?
- How will conflicts of interest be recognised and managed within the consortium? Board members have a duty to put the organisation's interests first, but in reality they may be affected by decisions such as how business is divided up between consortium members.
- Will the consortium deliver any services directly or will it all be subcontracted out to its members?

All of these points need to be resolved before any bidding rounds begin. Any consortium bid must show that processes and procedures for how the consortium will operate are robust, clearly documented and understood by all.

Competition law

In choosing to set up or be involved in a consortium, attention should be given to the possible impact of European and UK competition law. Competition law aims to prevent activities and agreements that could prevent, restrict or distort competition. Such anti-competitive behaviour includes:

- price fixing, i.e. providers operating as a cartel and agreeing a minimum price;
- bid rigging, such as parties agreeing to take turns in bidding;
- removal of competition or limiting competition to a closed group of providers.

Competition law is complex. The Office of Fair Trading, which oversees the application of competition law, produces some useful information material on fair competition (see further reading on page 140). Furthermore, in designing a consortium, it is advisable to take specialist legal advice to ensure that it is established in a way that is open, transparent and designed to operate in a way that does not restrict competition.

Success factors

Setting up and choosing to work in a consortium is a significant step. The following seven factors are likely to be critical to a consortium's long-term success.

1. **Organisational buy-in.** The organisations that choose to join the consortium and become members must understand the idea and not simply see it as a mechanism to get funding. Organisations must be willing to commit time to the consortium, be prepared to be accountable to other consortium members and occasionally accept that the consortium might be best placed to bid for something rather than bidding on their own.

2. **Commissioner's support.** Time should be taken to ensure that the consortium fits with the commissioner's procurement rules and requirements and that commissioners can see the value and gain of having a consortium structure.

3. **Start-up finance.** There will be a cost involved in creating a new structure and in developing it. It might be possible to meet these costs by bidding for grants or by securing loans, or member organisations might need to be levied to cover these costs.

4. **An entrepreneurial spirit.** The leadership members of the consortium must be skilled at marketing and business development. They need to be able to identify possible markets, recognise opportunities and ensure that the consortium has a strong and positive profile with prospective and current commissioners.

5. **Fairness and transparency.** As a membership organisation, there must be clear and fair mechanisms for sharing out contracts, monitoring delivery and admitting new members into the consortium. The consortium must work in an open way. It is not a cabal or a cartel!

6. **Long-term commitment.** Setting up a new structure takes time. It also takes time to explain the concept and ensure that the consortium is bid-ready. Members need to be able to stick with it and see it as a longer-term commitment.

7. **A durable market.** For a consortium to be viable in the medium to longer term, it must analyse its current and future markets and make a judgement about the likely size of the market and the best- and worst-case opportunities for the consortium and its members. Is the market big enough to generate enough business to keep the consortium and its members in work? Is diversifying into other markets viable? Ideally, a consortium should be able to show its value by opening up new markets and thereby increasing the flow of work to its member organisations.

The real test of a consortium is likely to be its ability to bring in new income streams to its members that enable them to deliver better services which meet users' and communities' needs.

Joint ventures

This model involves the partners creating a new and separate body to deliver a service. The partner organisations will usually have ownership and control of the new body and be represented on its board. A key feature of a joint venture that differentiates it from a bidding consortium is that it delivers services directly to users. The new body will deliver services and employ staff and work alongside the partners.

Examples of joint ventures include:

- a group of social care providers setting up and controlling a new company to deliver a workforce training and development function;
- three local agencies setting up a new structure to jointly own and manage a central resource centre from which they would all operate.

A typical joint venture structure

This model, illustrated in figure 6.2, involves the parties agreeing to create and run a new venture. It also means that they delegate some activities to the new venture. The member organisations are represented on the joint venture's board.

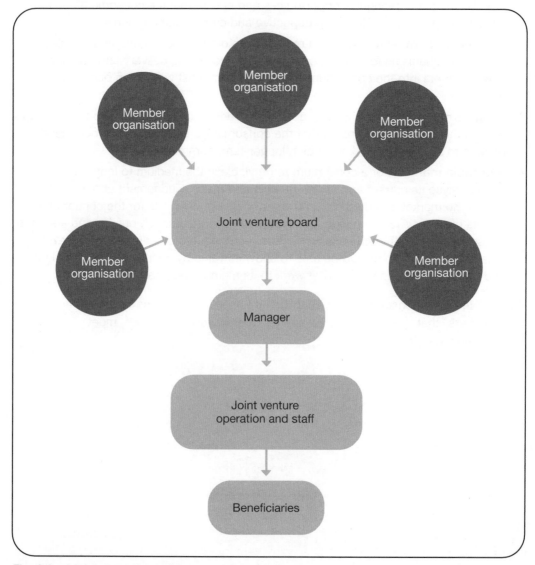

Fig. 6.2   A joint structure model.

In a joint venture, parties play the following roles:

	Role	Critical issues
Member organisations	Members choose to join the joint venture organisation. They appoint the board and work alongside the joint venture's staff.	Members need to accept that some things will be done on a collective level. They must be willing to put some staff time into the joint venture. The joint venture must develop a way of working which ensures that member organisations feel part of the venture and know what is happening.
Joint venture board	The board has the overall responsibility for managing the operation. Its members are responsible for the proper operation of the organisation as set out in the consortium's governing document.	Board members must accept that they are obliged to act in the best interest of the joint venture and not simply represent their organisation.
Joint venture manager	The manager is the principal employee of the joint venture and is directed by the board. The manager oversees all the operations and reports to the board.	The manager has a critical role. The manager must agree with the board-delegated areas of responsibility.
Joint venture staff	The staff are managed by the manager. They deliver the services and carry out the operational tasks.	Staff will need the cooperation of the staff of member organisations in order to deliver their work.

Working in a joint venture involves managing at a distance. Member organisations need to be able to agree and accept that some activities will be carried out by the joint venture rather than by their organisation. Not everything can be resolved by discussions and debate at meetings. Staff employed by the joint venture must be able to get on with the work and be clear about what decisions they can make. Agreeing the following issues can help:

● What are the key policy and strategic issues that must be dealt with by the joint venture's governing body?

● What decisions can be delegated to the joint venture's manager?

● How will the joint venture's manager be supervised and supported?

● How will disagreements between joint venture members be resolved?

Joint ventures can give an activity a real focus and identity. They work best when they have a clear scope that fits with and complements the work and activities of the member organisations. Setting up a joint venture structure can take time, so it is important that there is a long-term need for it and a long-term commitment from people in the member organisations to give time to it and make it work.

Joint venture case studies

A shared venture

The idea of sharing a resource centre between three different organisations seemed like a clear winner. After a series of successful bids, sufficient funds were obtained to purchase a building owned by a newly created company that was set up by the three organisations. The organisations would be able to be located in a convenient town-centre space and it was hoped that by working together they would be able to deliver a broad and connected range of services that none of them could do separately. The company's board would be made up of two representatives from each of the three organisations and it would oversee the building. The three organisations had agreed to jointly employ a building manager with one organisation acting as the formal employer.

Six months after the centre's opening, problems began to develop. There were clear differences as to how the organisations worked. One prided itself on being very organised and businesslike. Another was 'more relaxed about timekeeping and other organisational matters'.

At her three-monthly review, the new building manager expressed her frustration at working for three quite different organisations: 'I get conflicting messages about what's important. At times I feel everybody is in charge and at the same time no one is. '

The centre's board was clearly struggling with its role. It frequently avoided making decisions and at times seemed more like a forum for each organisation to make its points about how the centre was operating from its point of view.

At the prompting of the manager, the board held a special awayday to discuss the issue and came up with a four-point action plan that has made some progress in resolving the issues:

1. The role of the board is to govern and manage the centre overall. Members of the board are there as directors and not as representatives of their organisations.

2. An independent person would be recruited to chair the board to help it to operate.

3. One member of the board would be nominated to provide line management and supervision of the centre manager. The supervisor is intended to provide support and guidance to the centre manager and also to help resolve problems between user organisations.

4. The board would draw up a short document of centre-wide operating standards that all organisations would be asked to sign up to.

These steps are leading to a more consistent and coherent approach from all of the partners in how they run the building.

⚙ Joint venture case studies *cont.*

Who's in charge? A new way of working ⚙

The coordinator of a training project run by five voluntary organisations as a joint venture described some of the issues he encountered in his first year:

The organisations that made up the joint venture were very keen for it to work. Nevertheless, with hindsight, it is obvious that each organisation had a different view of how it should work and what my priorities should be.

It was agreed that I would be line managed by the Director of one of the organisations. The problem with this was twofold. First, she had a demanding job in her own organisation and, realistically, the project and providing supervision of me kept sliding down her to-do list. Secondly, she was not clear what decisions she could make and what had to go to the project management group. Often quite routine decisions, like buying a photocopier, would have to wait for a management group meeting.

The people who made up the management group were very concerned that the consortium didn't favour one particular organisation. This led to a reluctance to delegate clearly. They would often get involved in day-to-day operational issues. They would often struggle to reach an agreement as they debated 'the best way to do something'. This started to affect our ability to deliver.

It has taken us a long time to build up trust between members. In some cases work on the joint venture, such as attending meetings or drafting our governing document, was seen by some as time away from their job in their own organisation. We have started to turn a corner. We now have a plan that is actively supported and owned by the managers. We have started to build a style of work that is more collective and ensures that there is good communication within the project and also regular report-back sessions to the member organisations.

I don't think that we really recognised that working in this way would require such a different approach. People have to be able to delegate and sometimes accept that their way of doing something might not be the only way. To work in a joint venture managers have to be able to think and operate beyond the boundaries of their own organisation. In the start-up phase, the work involved in setting the joint venture up is unlikely to create an immediate payback, but members must be prepared to be in it for the longer term.

⚙ Joint venture case studies *cont.*

Liverpool Specialist Advice Services ⚙

Liverpool Specialist Advice Services (LSAS) is an independent charitable company set up by Citizens Advice Bureaux in Liverpool in 1998 originally to bid for and manage legal services contracts in Liverpool.

LSAS has an annual turnover of around £1.3 million and employs a small core team responsible for bidding for contracts and coordinating and supporting service delivery. LSAS does not deliver advice itself. The delivery is carried out by individual bureaux throughout the city. LSAS's role and expertise is in contract management and in coordinating service delivery.

In reviewing LSAS's development and growth the following features are worth noting:

- LSAS moved from being a project to being an organisation in its own right. LSAS is now a fully constituted organisation with its own governance, staff and structures. This gives it the credibility and track record to bid for contracts in its own right.

- Originally the managers of the individual bureaux that founded LSAS made up the LSAS governing board. A decision was taken to recruit new and independent board members. Having independent board members brings a fresh perspective to the organisation and avoids potentially conflicting interests between being an LSAS board member and the manager of a service that delivers contracts.

- LSAS had to develop and agree clear procedures, agreements and sanctions to govern the relationship between LSAS and its partners. At its inception, it relied upon trust and goodwill between partners. Whilst this has remained, formal and written agreements are needed to govern a major service delivery operation.

- LSAS needs to synchronise its plans and future business development with those of its member bureaux. There is regular discussion and consultation about what LSAS should bid for and what individual bureaux are best placed to go for.

- There needs to be a culture of openness and transparency in how the organisation works. People need to know what is going on and how decisions are made, and be involved in the process throughout.

Rachel Howley, LSAS's manager commented that 'building and establishing an effective consortium depends very much on how partners communicate with each other. As well as formal agreements, in my experience, having agreed principles on communication is essential to positive and long-lasting relationships within any collaboration.'

Joint venture case studies *cont.*

Sheffield Well-being Consortium

Sheffield Well-being Consortium was established to ensure that voluntary and community organisations did not miss out on health-based commissioning opportunities. The consortium now has over seventy members. All members must meet certain membership criteria which include an externally validated minimum quality-assurance threshold. The consortium is constituted as a registered company limited by guarantee and a registered charity.

So far the consortium has been successful in winning a number of health-related contracts including a Health Champions programme and hosting a programme to deliver the government's Improving Access to Psychological Therapies initiative. The consortium has also been able to establish through contract income a small core staff team of a director and a business manager to lead and develop the consortium and two staff to support the work on community champions.

The consortium has adopted a hub and spoke model with member organisations making up the majority of the consortium's board (the hub is the central infrastructure or staff resource that acts as the executive engine of Sheffield Well-being Consortium, including negotiating and subletting contracts, while the spokes are the various individual member organisations/providers). Sheffield Well-being Consortium hub has a small staff team with a range of duties: leadership, negotiation, tender writing, contract management, resource allocation, quality improvement and organisational capacity building. Generally, the hub not only ensures smooth and efficient contract management, but also proactively seeks out new funding and business development opportunities on behalf of the membership and works to develop the market for third-sector providers.

As well as its financial/business development brief, the hub is tasked with building the capacity of member organisations through network events and training.

Future plans

Key future priorities for the consortium are:

- to ensure the financial sustainability of the consortium by diversifying income and generating income from contracts and consultancy;
- to increase turnover so that more funding can be distributed to members to deliver frontline services;
- to develop into other areas including the potential for direct payments (i.e. where service users directly control or purchase a service);
- to continue to raise the profile of Sheffield Well-being Consortium through marketing and showing the social return on investment for contracts delivered;
- building the capacity of the consortium's membership.

Cont.

Sheffield Well-being Consortium *cont.*

The consortium's director, Mandy Forrest, commented on their experience so far:

Whilst statutory and funding bodies say they want a well-prepared third sector to provide innovative services on the ground, and in theory recognise the added value of working with a consortium of organisations, in reality commission, procurement and contracting processes struggle to enable this to happen.

A key risk is that commissioners want the third sector to transform without any support from commissioners, either in terms of market development or financial support to enable this change.

Chapter seven
Group structures

A group structure is a constitutional and governance arrangement whereby a number of organisations decide to join together but retain a level of individual identity and operation. Group structures have their roots in the commercial world, where a group is a cluster of legally distinct firms with a managerial relationship. In a group structure, a parent organisation governs a group of subsidiary organisations which retain their own legal identities.

In this type of structure, organisation A becomes the holding company for organisations B and C. Organisation A has the controlling governance powers over organisations B and C (see fig. 7.1). Organisations B and C continue to operate, but are subsidiaries of organisation A.

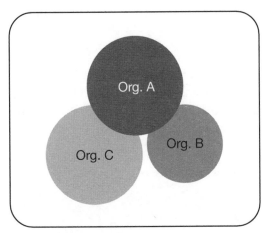

Fig. 7.1 A group structure.

Group structures have become quite common in the housing association movement where they have been formed to allow and encourage growth and diversity. A recent example in the voluntary sector is the Royal National Institute of Blind People (RNIB), which has developed a group structure under which Action for Blind People and the Cardiff Institute for the Blind have joined RNIB, but continue operating under their own name and identity. Under the structure used, RNIB is the sole shareholder of its affiliates. RNIB's Chief Executive, Lesley Anne Alexander, describes a group structure as 'somewhere between collaboration and merger or takeover' (Plummer 2009).

Group structures vary in terms of structure and design, but usually have the following features:

- One member of the group is the constitutional 'parent'. It has ultimate control of group members and their assets.
- All of the group members have similar (but not necessarily identical) aims and are focused on the same beneficiaries.
- Groups can be made up of different sorts of organisations: registered charities, trading companies and community interest companies.
- Some activities and decisions are carried out at a group level.
- Group members usually retain their own name and identity, but acknowledge their membership of the group brand.
- The group will usually produce consolidated accounts.

Advocates of group structures would suggest that being a member of a group structure can offer some advantages:

- **Being a bigger player.** A group structure can help organisations move onto a bigger stage without fully merging. For smaller organisations, coming together in a group structure could lead to having a higher profile and possibly the size and scale to be able to go for bigger contracts.

- **Keeping your identity.** A group structure allows members to retain the identity and profile that they have built up in their locality or community.

- **Having safety in numbers.** A group can offer financial security. Being a part of a bigger organisation might reduce business risk and open up new sources of income. The group may have the size and diversity of business operations to manage cash flow, invest in new ideas and provide working capital that the individual organisations do not have on their own.

- **Offering organisational diversity.** A group structure can offer greater diversity; for example, a housing group could operate a range of Registered Social Landlords, a charity promoting strong communities and a community interest company offering homecare support services.

- **Providing stronger management.** Being part of a group can provide access to a range of in-house services that organisations on their own could not afford. The group might be able to offer central services such as human resources, training, marketing and business development that individual members would struggle to do if they were on their own.

- **Offering support and sharing.** A group structure should be able to provide opportunities for staff to develop their skills, learn from each other and move within the group.

On the negative side, there is some concern that group structures can create governance and decision-making processes that are overly complex and centralised, and make local involvement and engagement of users and communities difficult. There is a danger of the potential benefits being lost, as too much attention goes into creating a management structure to run and control the group's activities.

Case study: group support

The Director of a small specialist housing association described her experience of becoming part of a group structure:

We recognised that being on our own as an independent organisation was becoming increasingly hard. It was a struggle to keep going. Becoming part of a group structure gave us the back-up and access to specialist technical expertise that we would not be able to have on our own. Although we are owned by the group and accountable to it, we do have a significant degree of autonomy to operate as we see best. When there is a problem, usually there is someone in the group that we can call on for advice and help. The group also gives us an increased level of financial security and credibility.

At times we have worried about losing our independence and ending up as a small part of a large organisation. Over time we have managed to reach a working agreement about what we can do and what has to be approved by the group. A key factor is that the group's chief executive is very clear about what he needs to control and that he is comfortable to delegate most business and operational issues to the individual organisations that make up the group.

Working in a group structure

In researching this book, a number of trustees and managers identified five factors that seem to be critical success factors in getting a group structure to work:

1. Agreement on which functions can be done best at group level

Certain activities are best done at a group level and other activities are best managed and organised at a subordinate level. One successful group structure decided that the most sensible way to manage financial control, strategic planning, new business and policy advocacy was centrally by the group on behalf of the group members. Other activities became the responsibility of members. An experienced manager commented:

In the past we have had quite lively debates about 'what has to go to group'. At times the group was seen as being controlling, risk-averse and wanting to micro-manage issues. We have worked through that issue and are much clearer about the issues and decisions that need to be resolved at local level or that can be best determined at group level.

2. Group brand identity

Although member organisations retain their name and identity, there needs to be an acknowledgement that the organisation is a member of the group. Developing a simple strapline and identity can promote the group and retain local identity.

3. Shared vision across the group

There needs to be a common sense of purpose that connects all the group's activities and operations. Where and how services are delivered will be diverse and varied, but there must be a shared vision which connects all the group's operations.

4. Shared values across the group

A key task for managers is creating a working style or culture that allows for differences across the group's activities, but has the same principles and ethos running throughout. One manager described how 'we have put a lot of time into encouraging and discussing shared values across the group – values are principled issues like how our users should be treated and respected. Our shared values hold the group together.'

5. The structure must be seen to be adding value

Being in a group structure is not about building an organisational structure. The role and purpose of the group structure is to enable the members to thrive, develop and meet their mission. The group will have a controlling role, but it must demonstrate that being part of the group adds more than it takes.

⚙ Case study: group structure in the HCT Group

The HCT group is an interesting example of an organisation that has developed a group structure model. Hackney Community Transport was set up in 1982 to enable 30 local community groups in the London Borough of Hackney to pool their vehicle resources.

It has grown from a handful of volunteers and a couple of minibuses with a turnover of £202,000 in 1993, to a large-scale social enterprise with more than 700 employees, ten depots spread across London, Yorkshire, Humberside and the South West, a fleet of over 340 vehicles and a 2010/11 turnover of £28.1 million. The group consists of four community interest companies, four registered charities, one industrial and provident society, three charitable companies and three joint ventures.

Its current structure is shown in figure 7.2.

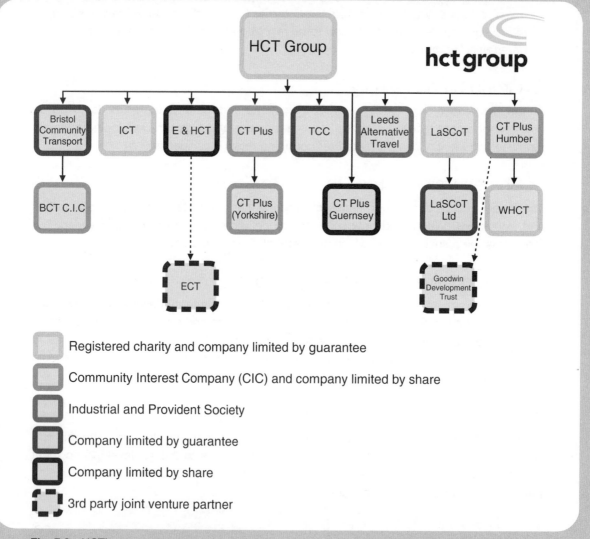

Registered charity and company limited by guarantee

Community Interest Company (CIC) and company limited by share

Industrial and Provident Society

Company limited by guarantee

Company limited by share

3rd party joint venture partner

Fig. 7.2 HCT's group structure and legal forms

HCT has a controlling share in each of the local organisations. This provides an 'asset lock' (a legal clause which prevents the assets of a company (income or capital) being used for private gain) to ensure that all resources or profit generated can only be used for charitable purposes. Each organisation operates its own services with a strapline showing that they are part of HCT.

As well as providing an overall level of accountability and coordination centrally, the group provides three core functions for group organisations:

1. financial management;
2. marketing and communications;
3. the management of large-scale new projects and major development bids.

Chief Executive Dai Powell described the evolution of the structure:

> *The HCT Group structure has evolved in direct response to our business needs. As those needs change, our group structure is likely to change with them. We believe that structure should never stop a social enterprise doing what it needs to do. Yet even in the face of change and evolution, our group structure will always have one constant – the asset lock at its heart that means we exist solely for community benefit.*

Being part of a group gives HCT's local organisations several advantages:

- **The group is greater than the sum of its parts**. Individual community transport operations benefit from being part of a bigger commercial operation. The group structure brings a level of management and business skills and resources that individual operators would not usually have access to.
- **Each organisation becomes a bigger player but still retains a local identity.** The group has developed ways and structures to ensure that local operations still remain in touch with their local communities and has developed processes for local people to be involved. At the same time, being part of a larger group gives it the capacity to bid successfully against larger commercial operators for contracts.
- **Each organisation is part of a bigger brand.** The group has the ability to influence transport policy and develop a wider brand identity on a national scale. Individual operators would not have the time or opportunity to do this on their own.
- **There are opportunities to share experience in the brand.** The group is developing processes to share skills and expertise across the brand.

HCT delegates most management decisions to managers in individual group organisations. For it to work overall, the group has to retain a strong sense of core values that links together all of its operations.

Chapter eight
Mergers

Introduction

In the voluntary sector, the decision for organisations to merge is sometimes seen as a last resort. Many of the different forms of collaboration described earlier in this book will have been tried by organisations before a merger is considered. In some cases, it might be working together in partnerships and consortia that has paved the way for formal merger discussions. Sometimes it will be a crisis in one or other of the merging organisations that puts the issue on the agenda. However an organisation comes to it, the decision to merge should not be taken lightly, and before considering a merger, trustees should always have considered the alternatives.

In many cases, the decision to merge comes about because an organisation believes that the best way it can secure its future and the services it offers is by merging with another organisation. A survey undertaken by the Charity Commission (2003) reported that the most common reasons for merging were: 'to increase efficiency (54%); as a way of rescuing a charity in difficulties (44%); and to prevent duplication or to improve services (42%)'.

This chapter explores the definition of mergers in the not-for-profit sector, different types of mergers, motivations for merging and the experience from elsewhere of mergers. It looks at the key questions to ask when considering a merger and provides practical guidance on how to bring a merger about.

Why merge?

In the commercial world, companies merge in order to save costs, increase profits and improve services. In the voluntary sector, motivations for merging are more complex and can be brought about by a number of factors, including a financial crisis (immediate or impending), the departure of the existing chief executive, a proactive move to reduce competition or a request from another organisation.

The catalyst is often the need to maintain and improve services to the beneficiaries in a tougher funding climate, and this can be harder to quantify. Over the past several years an increasing issue is the external pressure to merge:

> There has been a view amongst the general public that there are too many charities, or too many operating in a particular field with similar aims: for example, the Charity Commission's survey of Public Attitudes in 1999 found that a majority of those questioned felt that there were too many charities. While in the private sector competing providers are often seen as offering consumer choice and lower prices, in the voluntary sector the existence of a range of agencies doing broadly

similar work can be seen as wasteful duplication. This is especially the case if they are competing for the same constrained funding pots, e.g. Lottery money, a charitable foundation or local individual donors. These trends throw the spotlight on how voluntary organisations are managed and there is an expectation that they will be efficient and effective, especially when they receive funding from government agencies.

Cairns, Harris & Hutchinson 2003

This view has become more prevalent recently as the government seeks to reduce the public sector deficit. In some areas, local authority cuts by central government have hit the voluntary sector disproportionately because local authorities look much harder at the services the sector is providing. Whilst in some cases this has led to reductions in voluntary sector budgets, in others, organisations have moved to a reconfiguring of services with pressure to put more money into frontline delivery and find more innovative (and cheaper) ways to deliver services.

Commissioning is also being used much more widely to bring about change. Whilst in the past public bodies may have bemoaned duplication in the sector, now they are being much more proactive in stating that they will only fund one organisation and one set of organisational costs. As one local authority officer put it: 'funding three sets of management costs, three sets of running costs and paying for three sets of premises for the delivery of similar services is a luxury we can no longer afford. We want one contract and one set of overheads.'

The success criteria for a merger

A useful way of gaining and testing support for a merger is to develop some success criteria for what a merged organisation will be able to do and offer. The criteria are best drawn up by asking people how they will know if the merger has been a success a year or so after it has happened. They should look at both hard factors (tangible and easy-to-measure results) and soft factors (perceptions, morale and atmosphere).

Drawing up the success criteria is a useful tool for involving people who might have an interest in the merger and developing a positive vision of what is possible in a merged organisation.

The joint working group of two environmental charities developed the following success criteria as a result of their merged talks.

The merger will have been a success if . . .

Hard factors

- we maintain our current level of services and develop others;
- we are able to win new contracts;
- we retain our staff;
- we have retained support from most of our volunteers and charitable donors;
- we are able to develop new businesses and income streams;
- our combined management and overhead costs reduce or stay the same.

Soft factors

- our users still see the service as being local and relevant to their needs;
- our funders and commissioners remain supportive;
- communication, teamwork and practice-sharing is good across the organisation;
- the organisation has a strong, positive and forward-looking identity.

It is worth sounding a note of caution here about the level of savings and improvements in services that can be made by merging:

> *Many of the surveyed charities did not experience significant improvements after merger. 6% of surveyed charities stated that their administrative costs had actually increased following a merger, but they stayed the same for the majority of charities (39%). 30% reported that the level of service delivery had stayed the same as a result of the merger and only 9% reported that their ability to compete for funding had improved.*
>
> *These figures demonstrate that common assumptions about reduced overheads and increased ability to raise funds and provide services are not necessarily borne out in practice. Each situation needs to be evaluated on its own merits.*
>
> Charity Commission 2003

Whilst one reason for merging in the new climate of competitive commissioning can be to reduce competition for scarce resources, another reason for merger is to increase the 'share of the pie' that voluntary organisations can gain access to. The last few years have seen a desire by successive governments for more services to be commissioned from not-for-profit organisations. In order for voluntary organisations to be able to compete and deliver public service contracts effectively, there has been a real need to provide organisations' staff with additional skills and develop a management infrastructure that is business-orientated and able to deal with the demands of managing large contracts. In many cases, the only way this can be done is by merging with other organisations that have similar aims and objectives.

However, it is important that organisations do not merge just to satisfy external pressures or to be able to compete for contracts more effectively. Whilst these pressures are very real, a decision to merge needs to be underpinned by a belief that the merger will enable the organisation to fulfil its aims and meet the needs of its beneficiaries more effectively. Examples of this may be that the merged organisation can:

- reach more beneficiaries;
- have an increased public profile;
- reduce costs and duplication, freeing up resources for service delivery;
- improve the client experience by sharing experiences and developing new and better ways of working.

Regardless of how the question of merging arises, the question to answer is always the same – will it help our beneficiaries and increase the stability of the organisation?

The following list (reproduced from *Charity Mergers: Tackling the issues in practice*) shows how the respondents to a questionnaire collectively ranked various motivations or 'drivers' to merge. However, recent anecdotal evidence suggests that 9, 10 and 13 may be creeping higher up the list.

Ranking of drivers to merger

1. *Provision of wider, more consistent service*
2. *Increased campaigning influence*
3. *Better geographical reach*
4. *Increased capacity to fundraise*
5. *Access to contracts*
6. *Reduced overheads*
7. *History of successful collaboration*
8. *Government/Local Authority encouragement*
9. *Prevent duplication of service*
10. *Rescue merger*
11. *Public perception*
12. *Access to Trustees*
13. *Pressure from funders*

Social Finance 2009

What is a merger?

The following definitions are a useful starting point:

A merger can be considered to involve the coming together of two or more organisations, all their assets and liabilities to form one new body, with a single name, legal form, governing body and mission. This may or may not be achieved by one organisation 'acquiring' another, or by one or all organisations 'dissolving'.

Cairns, Harris and Hutchison 2003

The Charity Commission definition clarifies it thus:

A merger of charities means two or more separate charities coming together to form one organisation. Either a new charity is formed to continue the work or take on the assets of the charities, or one charity assumes control of the other.

Charity Commission 2009

An organisation's governing documents will usually contain the powers needed to allow an organisation to merge with another, either through a dissolution clause or an express power to merge. However, to ensure that the merger is done in the best interests of the charities' intended beneficiaries, the objects (or purposes) of the merging organisations should be compatible. So, for example, if one charity's objects are much broader than those of the other, steps would need to be taken to make sure that the assets of the charity with the wider objects would not be limited (and therefore some beneficiaries it was founded to help, not helped).

With this in mind, it is crucial to have or to create compatible objects for a merger to be successful and so this is an obvious starting point in any potential merger discussion. Note this does not mean that the purposes need to be identical. If trustees are concerned, however, that those of either the newly merged organisation or the charity to which they intend to transfer could be regarded as being significantly different, but they feel that there are still strong reasons to merge, advice should be taken from the Charity Commission. The Commission can provide advice early in the process on both the charitable objects and the constitutional issues. However, most mergers do not require Charity Commission consent.

The most common forms of merger in the not-for-profit sector are undertaken by:

1. using the existing structures of one of the merging organisations; or

2. forming a completely new organisation.

Where an existing structure is used, one organisation is wound up and passes its assets to the other (see fig. 8.1). When a new organisation is formed, all the organisations transfer their assets to a new organisation with similar objects and the original organisations wind up (see fig. 8.2).

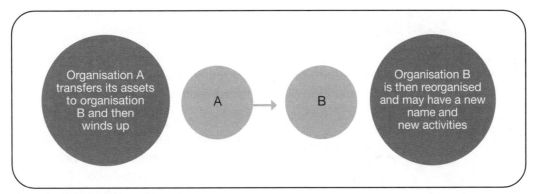

Fig. 8.1 Using existing structures

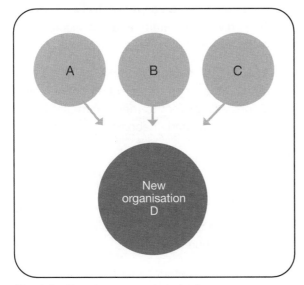

Fig. 8.2 Creating a new organisation

Types of merger

In commercial mergers and acquisitions the terms 'horizontal mergers' and 'vertical mergers' are used to describe two different ways of building post-merged organisations.

A horizontal merger is where organisations doing similar work join forces and create a new and bigger organisation (see fig. 8.3).

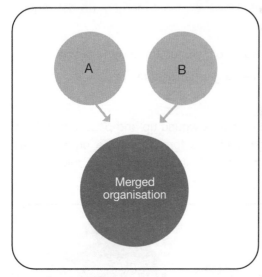

Fig. 8.3   Horizontal merger

A horizontal merger is usually about aggregating together and becoming a bigger and stronger force. It might produce savings, particularly by cutting out some duplication and by having the same overhead functions working across a bigger service delivery.

An example of a horizontal merger in the voluntary sector is two neighbouring organisations that do roughly the same work with a similar client group merging into one single organisation.

A vertical merger is where one organisation takes over another organisation and takes it into its structures (see fig. 8.4).

In a vertical merger, organisation B ceases to be a separate legal entity and transfers its activities to organisation A. It becomes a constituent part of organisation A. Vertical mergers might give organisation A the ability to take on specialist functions or to expand its areas of activity. It might also give the staff and services from organisation B a more secure future.

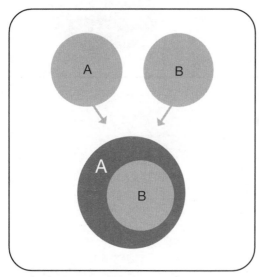

Fig. 8.4   Vertical merger

A voluntary sector example of a vertical merger is a larger organisation encouraging a specialist project to merge into that larger organisation and become a department of it.

The form a merger takes will depend on the organisations' governing documents, what they need the merged organisation to do and how the case for merger has been presented. Sometimes, creating a new charity can help the merger process, as it can be used to avoid the merger looking like a takeover or 'rescue' merger.

More positively, it can signal a new approach and a new start by all the organisations involved in the merger, and it can help to create a break with the past.

It is possible to characterise four types of merger, and often the type of merger will signal the form the merger will take. Most mergers include at least one of the following characteristics, and some can include elements of all four.

1. A rescue mission

A rescue mission usually happens when one party feels that it can no longer continue to struggle on and believes that it will only survive by merging with another party. An example of this is when an organisation decides that it is no longer viable and decides to transfer what is left of its assets into another, hopefully stronger, organisation.

2. A takeover

A takeover is when one party is invited to become part of another, usually stronger, body in the hope that they will be able to do their work better as one organisation. Several takeovers have occurred because a smaller organisation is seen as lacking the management resources and organisational capacity to continue in a tough and competitive environment. However, it is worth noting that with charities, a takeover still requires the consent of the smaller organisation. There is no direct equivalent of the 'hostile takeovers' sometimes found in commercial situations where one company buys a large portion of the shares of a smaller company in order to take it over, against the wishes of its board.

3. A defensive manoeuvre

A defensive manoeuvre is when organisations recognise that they need to operate collectively to defend themselves against some kind of external threat. An example of this is a group of local charities merging into the national charity, after recognising that future commissioning rounds were likely to bring in new national competitors. Becoming one national charity enables them to bid for parts of a larger pie.

4. A new start

A new start is when organisations see an opportunity to develop their services in a positive way by merging with other organisations. The initiative is a proactive one, designed to improve the way that they meet their objectives and help their beneficiaries.

Case study: it's not about me

Gordon, the original founder, first paid worker and then director of a housing charity, described how he realised that the organisation had to consider significant opportunities which might work against his personal interests.

In many ways the charity is part of me. I set it up and have been its main driving force. For the past three months we have had some options about working with other agencies on the table. A national housing association has suggested that we become part of their group structure. A similarly sized local agency has floated the possibility of a merger. There's also a possibility of becoming part of a bidding consortium to go after larger social care contracts.

To be honest, I have been stalling on all of these. I can see that, done properly, they could create a more secure future than sticking it out on our own, but I am not the person to carry them through. I have too much of a personal investment in the organisation. I would not be able to work as the number two on someone else's management team! Me staying here will block proper consideration of these issues. A key part of leadership is to know when it's time to go.

The financial implications of a merger

Mergers are often driven by financial considerations, with the idea that a merger will help lower costs and create savings by reducing duplication and having an economy of scale. Three different types of financial implications appear in a merger:

1. Direct savings caused by mergers.
2. Direct expenses incurred in the merger process.
3. Additional costs of being a larger merged organisation.

1. Direct savings caused by mergers

The process of merging could take out some organisational costs. By combining organisations it should be possible to identify some savings caused by reducing duplication. Examples include:

A possible reduction in some central management costs

- Only having one chief executive.
- Only needing one head office.

Direct efficiency savings

- Only needing one set of audited accounts, annual report and other costs associated with being a separate organisation.
- Reducing costs by integrating services: only one person having to carry out a task rather than two people from two organisations doing it.

A better use of resources

- Resources being better used. Organisation A has two minibuses and organisation B has three. In both organisations the minibuses are only used to around 70% of their available capacity. A and B merge and by centralising transport only need four minibuses.

2. Direct expenses incurred in the merger process

The process of merging will probably incur some one-off transitional costs. These costs could include those of:

- obtaining expert advice;
- time and expenses of staff and trustees involved in considering the merger;
- communication with stakeholders;
- integrating or adapting IT systems.
- setting up new structures and closing old ones.
- any staff reorganisation: severance and redundancy costs;
- redundancy costs if the merged organisation will have a slimmed down staff;
- launching and branding the new merged organisation;
- running a multi-site organisation;
- post-merger integration, such as induction events and producing a single set of procedures for the new organisation.

Transitional and start-up costs should usually be budgeted and accounted for separately.

The issue of staff pensions needs to be explored early in the merger process. The new merged organisation or the receiving organisation may well be faced with a significant pension liability caused by having to take over existing staff pensions or having to compensate a pension fund. This issue, together with the pensions deficit faced by many pension funds, is an important one and in some cases has stalled the merger process. Full and proper professional advice needs to be taken on the pensions position early in the process. (See page 121 for more information on pensions.)

A trustee of a housing charity described her experience: 'We were ready to sign on the dotted line and then we found out that to merge could trigger a huge pension liability which would transfer to the new organisation. This should have been identified at the due diligence stage.' (See page 114 for an explanation of due diligence.)

3. Additional costs of being a larger merged organisation

On becoming a larger organisation there could be an increase in some administrative and overhead costs as a result of organisations combining and becoming a larger single organisation. As organisations become bigger, overhead costs can be inclined to increase as the need for new and dedicated roles in functions such as IT support and human resources becomes obvious.

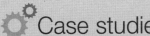 Case studies: creeping costs

The treasurer of a local children's charity described his experience:

We looked at all kinds of possible savings by merging with a similar organisation. We kind of assumed that we would be able to make savings in overhead costs. This proved not to be the case as both organisations had very small and under-resourced core and management costs. We both spent so little on management that it was impossible to see how anything could be sensibly cut out. If anything, the merger exposed that we needed to invest more in our management costs.

The finance officer of a newly merged health charity commented:

I try to keep this quiet, but since merging our organisational costs have started to creep up. Pre-merger, both organisations had around 25 to 30 staff. Now as a single organisation with 60 staff we seem to have moved into a different level of operation. We need bigger and quicker financial systems. Managers need better support in personnel, marketing and facilities management. To respond to this we have had to create additional management roles.

More positively, the director of a merged organisation outlined her experience:

Direct savings were relatively small. What has made a difference is that merging gave us the opportunity to design things afresh and also it has freed up some staff time by reducing duplication (such as two people attending the same meeting or doing similar work in two separate organisations) that has enabled us to redirect staff time to things that are important to us like new service development, but were often neglected as managers spent their time struggling to run separate day-to-day operations.

The role of trustees in the merger process

No one can make an organisation merge. The final decision to merge has to be taken by the board of an organisation and cannot be delegated. There is no such thing as a hostile takeover in the not-for-profit sector and each board involved in a merger has the independent authority to make its choice. Whilst, in practice, the discussions about a merger often start between the senior employees of the organisations, the discussions need to be widened at an early stage to include the trustees, and a decision from the board will be required to enable the discussions to move to a formal merger proposal.

It is important to remember that where an organisation has a membership, the members may have a right to vote for or against a merger proposal. Therefore, trustees will need to make sure that there is membership support for the proposal at an early stage.

Sayer Vincent and CFDG (2008) offer a useful list of questions that trustees must ask themselves:

- *Is merger really in the best interests of our beneficiaries? Why?*
- *Is there a better way of achieving the desired end result?*
- *Can we really work effectively with the merger partner?*
- *What will key stakeholders such as beneficiaries, funders, employees and volunteers think?*
- *What will be the costs of merger and how do these compare with the expected savings?*
- *How much time and effort is this going to take? What is the impact of this on service delivery?*
- *Are there any risks with the merger partner?*
- *If member consent is required – how are we going to obtain this?*
- *What if it all goes wrong?*

One trustee of an independent youth agency said that his organisation had considered merging with a neighbouring agency for a number of years. The fit was there, they shared a vision and indeed shared beneficiaries. However, he said that 'the decision to merge was only taken when there really was no alternative and it was increasingly likely that one or both would have to close if we didn't.' Other decisions to merge are, of course, more considered, as the following case study illustrates.

Case study: reframing the discussion

The chair of a community project described a major sea change in how her staff looked at the possibility of merging with a neighbouring organisation doing similar work.

The idea of merging has floated around for years. It would usually crop up as an opportunity or a threat at our annual trustee and staff awayday. It was often a somewhat negative or defensive discussion.

Last year there was a real shift in the discussion. A relatively new trustee asked people to discuss the idea from two perspectives:

1. *Would a merger work from an internal organisational perspective?*
2. *Would a merger work from the perspective of beneficiaries?*

Groups of staff and trustees worked on both questions. A brief summary of what they came up with is set out below:

Would a merger work from an internal organisational perspective?

- Putting two different staff teams together would be hard.
- Their conditions of employment and working practices are different.
- Their staff work differently from ours.
- We could lose our strong sense of teamwork. It's friendly here.
- We could get swallowed up.
- Our systems and processes are different.
- Would the new organisation need two managers and two admin teams?

Would a merger work from the perspective of beneficiaries?

- Being part of a bigger organisation could offer opportunities to develop new services and increase our reach.
- We could learn from each other and improve what we do.
- Being part of a bigger structure could mean that we would be able to win funding and contracts that we currently cannot get. So we could do more for clients.
- By combining we could offer a more holistic and accessible service.
- Being part of a bigger structure might mean we could develop more specialist services and develop more choice for users.

Despite the benefits to clients that staff identified, it was striking that many people's starting point was defending the status quo and in particular the ways of working that we had built up over the years. From some of the discussions it seemed that people were only interested in the internal organisational details of how a merger could work. At worst it felt that the people were more concerned about defending the organisation as it is rather than developing the service to users. We had to work really hard to reassure people that any interest in collaboration was about building better services for users and that by engaging in the bigger picture there was more chance of securing our future.

In moving the issue forward we have to ensure that we get things in the right order. First we have to focus on how collaboration could improve what we offer our users and strengthen our ability to work to our shared mission. Once that is clear, we can move on to plan out and manage the organisational detail and working implications.

Once the decision to merge has been taken in principle, the trustees have an important role in steering the process. If a merger project group or merger steering group is set up, then trustees from the merging organisations need to be included. Trustees should take a strategic view of the merger and use their distance from the day-to-day workings of the organisation to keep the focus on the long-term gains for the organisation. The purpose and vision of the new organisation need to be clearly understood and articulated. Trustees have a vital role to play in keeping these reasons in mind. Doing so will increase the chances of overcoming problems along the way.

Another vital role for the trustees is appointing the chief executive to the new organisation. This can be particularly difficult when the current post holders wish to be considered for the new position and where it is unlikely that there will be an alternative post in the new structure for the unsuccessful candidate. In these cases, it is imperative that trustees step up and take responsibility for navigating a fair process. Equally importantly, they must be willing to accept the result of that process even if their favoured candidate is unsuccessful.

Trustees can be influential in setting the tone for a merger. By being open and transparent and communicating decisions effectively, they can encourage a similar style of working throughout the organisation during the merger process.

Barriers to merging

Looking to merge organisations can sometimes trigger unexpected responses and it is interesting to try and identify what the barriers to a merger can be. The following table sets out some of the potential obstacles and barriers identified by Social Finance, along with some potential solutions or actions:

Potential obstacles/barriers	Potential solution or action
Time cost and resource constraints.	Grant or loan to cover cost. Internal staff movements. Engage interim staff. Engage external consultants.
Governance issues: • preservation of identity and brand; • duplication of chief executive and trustees; • decision-making powers/delays.	Most action would require buy-in from and negotiation with the merger partner, and therefore cannot be fully determined in advance. However, it would still be appropriate to have initial views in this regard to bring to the discussion.
Ego: preservation of autonomy and self-interest.	Robust business plan, outlining the relative merits of a merger. Frank, honest, open discussion and negotiation.
Funding: some funders might regard the newly merged organisation as having no track record. Also some funders will only support small/local organisations and the merged organisation may no longer qualify.	Early discussion with funders.

Cont.

Potential obstacles/barriers	Potential solution or action
Financial issues such as: ● pension issues; ● permanent endowment restrictions (see page 122).	Should be identified via upfront analysis and/or via the due diligence process. May require assistance from auditors and/or lawyers, and the Charity Commission. In the cases of difficult permanent endowment issues, legal advice from a charity law specialist is vital.
Legal considerations, for example: ● is a merger permitted under the current governing document? ● Any ongoing disputes.	Liaise with lawyers and the Charity Commission about making necessary amendments. Accelerate resolution of disputes.
Cultural fit.	Managers need to spend time helping to shape the new culture and build on the best of both.

Adapted from Social Finance 2009

Our experience of the voluntary sector is that staff, trustees and volunteers often have a great deal of personal investment in their organisation. These human factors can often be the biggest obstacle to merger. If one chief executive doesn't like their counterpart, it is highly unlikely that the merger will progress! Likewise with trustees.

Feelings of vulnerability and 'loss of empire' can also play a part. There can be a feeling that if the organisation merges it will lose its identity and, as a result, provide a lesser service to clients. Volunteers can sometimes be particularly hard to persuade of the benefits of a merger, particularly if they volunteer with the charity because it has helped them in the past or it is a locally based charity. They can sometimes feel that 'things won't be the same' if the organisation merges and becomes a larger organisation, or they may be concerned that they won't be able to volunteer in the same way or help people in their locality. Staff may feel insecure about their jobs and whether there is a job for them in the merged organisation, and they will react accordingly.

It can be very hard to convince people that the merger is about the charity, its beneficiaries and fulfilling its aims, and it requires skilled leadership to help people be objective about a process that will have a direct impact on them and their day-to-day lives.

To overcome these feelings of anxiety and scepticism, it is crucial to cultivate good lines of communication across the organisation. However, this does not just happen by itself. It needs to be managed actively and must be planned and organised at different levels: the trustee board, management and staff and the volunteers delivering the work. It should involve a range of techniques and encourage people to work together, explore what they have in common and what they can learn from each other. The objective of a communication plan is to oil the process, help people to understand each other and create channels and processes for dealing with some of the challenges ahead. For some tips on communicating the merger effectively see page 113.

The merger process

There is no set path for a merger and all mergers have their own unique elements. However, there are a number of steps that most mergers follow. Below is a typical merger process between charities, as outlined by the Charity Commission.

Trustees of each charity consider merger feasibility independently

This may cover costs, risks, and benefits to each charity.

Inform Charity Commission about merger proposal

The Commission can offer early advice on the legal/constitutional issues.

Form a project board or steering group

This should be made up of trustees and senior manager representatives with relevant skills from all charities involved. They will lead on negotiation and report back to respective trustees

Trustees commission formal due diligence exercise

This can be carried out in-house or by professional advisers. Trustees will need to determine the level of due diligence required

Trustees take formal decision to merge in light of due diligence exercise and inform Charity Commission of the decision

Appoint a project manager and project team

This is an operational team who keep oversight of the merger planning and communication. They should feedback to trustees regularly.

Charity Commission 2009

Within this overall process, there are a number of tasks that need to be undertaken and the following Gantt chart identifies the key tasks that may be involved in a merger process. These are not necessarily in order and not all tasks have to be completed before the formal merger is enacted. An early negotiation might be about what must be done pre-merger and what might be better left until a later date.

The table which follows the Gantt chart sets out some of the key activities involved in a merger process in more detail.

Example of a merger process and timescale

Task	1	2	3	4	5	6	7	8	9	10	11	12	13	14	15	16	17	18	19	20	21	22	23	24	25	26	27	28	29	30	31	32	33	34	35	36
Initial discussions																																				
Explore potential and gains	▓	▓	▓																																	
Discussions about future strategy		▓	▓	▓																																
Agree to move to formal considerations/in principle agreement				█																																
Get external advice				▓	▓																															
Set up joint group and plan merger process						▓	▓																													
Working group tasks																																				
Agree interim governance and staffing					▓																															
Plan legal structure										▓	▓	▓																								
Due diligence process									▓	▓	▓	▓																								
Plan staff transfers									▓	▓	▓	▓																								
Internal communications (staff, volunteers, users)			▓			▓	▓	▓	▓	▓	▓	▓																								
External communications (funders, partners)						▓	▓																													
Agree governance structure													▓	█																						
Agree service plan															█	▓																				
Enacting the merger																																				
Trustees agree to merge																		▓	█																	
Pass members resolution if needed																				█																
Register with the Charity Commission																				▓	▓	▓														
Register with Companies House																							▓	▓												
Transfer assets and properties																										▓	▓									
Wind up old organisation if necessary																							▓	▓												
Transfer staff																									▓	▓										
Agree transfer/novation of contracts																					▓	▓	▓													
Check VAT status																					▓	▓	▓													
File regulatory documents																					▓	▓	▓													
Notify suppliers and stakeholders																					▓	▓	▓													
Launch merged organisation																																				
Implement post-merger integration plan																																			▓	▓

■ **Key milestones/decisions:**

1. Agreement to move to formal consideration
2. Agreement to a feasibility study
3. Trustees agree to merge
4. Pass relevant resolution
5. Launch of merged organisation

Initial feasibility	Practical issues
Informal discussions between the organisations wishing to merge: can we work together successfully? What are the risks and benefits? Can we serve our beneficiaries better by merging? Will we be a more sustainable, stronger organisation?	These discussions are often initiated at a staff level but need to move to board level at an early stage.
An in-principle decision to explore a merger formally with the other parties is taken independently by each trustee board.	Each board must make its own decision. A simple outline of the business case can help the decision-making process.
If necessary, seek early advice on legal and constitutional issues relating to the merger from the Charity Commission.	Most organisations will have the power to merge within their memorandum and articles.
Formation of a merger working group to oversee the merger process and report back to trustee boards. This comprises representatives from the merging organisations and is usually a mixture of trustees, senior staff and independent advisors.	Can be useful to draw up a simple 'intent to merge' agreement. (See example on page 113.)
Tasks of the working group	
Agree interim governance and staffing arrangements.	This may include the appointment of an interim chief executive and/or a project manager to keep the merger process on track.
Reviews of governing documents: what legal form will the merger take?	The power to merge is in most organisations' governing documents. Where that isn't the case, contact the Charity Commission at an early stage.
Undertake due diligence processes.	(This is an essential part of the process which is outlined in more detail on page 114.)
Review contracts of employment: seek advice on TUPE and pension liabilities.	Expert advice on pension and TUPE liabilities is essential before proceeding to merger. (See also pages 120 and 121.)
Communicate with staff and volunteers.	Decisions are needed on when and how people should be communicated with.
Communicate with stakeholders and funders.	Decisions should be taken on when and how some stakeholders and funders need to be alerted at an early stage.
Agree governance structure for the merged organisation.	Who will chair the new organisation and who will be on the board?
Agree service delivery plan for the merged organisation.	What services will the new organisations deliver?
Agree staffing structure for the merged organisation.	Which staff structure will be needed to deliver the services? *Cont.*

Initial feasibility	Practical issues
Enacting the merger	
Pass trustee board resolutions formally agreeing the merger decision.	Advice on wording can be obtained from the Charity Commission.
Pass members resolutions if applicable.	If the organisation has members then they will be required to vote on the merger.
Register new charity with the Charity Commission or register changes to governing document.	Where a new charity has been formed or where changes have been made these will need to be registered.
Register the new company with Companies House or register changes to the memorandum and articles of association.	Where a new company has been formed or changes made to the memorandum and articles then these will need to be registered.
Enter into formal agreement to transfer assets to the new organisation or the transferee.	Trustees rely on the dissolution clause to transfer assets to the merged organisation. It is now also possible to use a vesting declaration. However, this will not always be suitable and advice should be sought on the best way forward.
Wind up organisations if a new entity is being formed or wind up the transferring organisation if it is a transfer.	
Transfer staff in accordance with TUPE regulations.	It is important to get this right. There are strict legal provisions that have to be followed when transferring staff. Legal advice should be sought.
Check the VAT status of the merged organisation.	The merger may take it over the relevant threshold.
File necessary documents with Companies House, the Charity Commission and other regulatory bodies such as Customs and Excise.	

Feasibility studies

A feasibility study is a tool used to pull together information, identify the potential costs and gains and help people to make informed decisions. A good feasibility study should look at the reasons for a proposal and test it out to explore potential risks, problems and weaknesses. It should also evaluate the potential benefits and gains that can be expected if the proposal goes ahead.

The study should be carried out in an impartial and objective way. It is usually useful to appoint an external consultant to do this as they are unlikely to have a longer-term stake in the process. A feasibility study does not make or even recommend the decision, rather it ensures that an idea has been tested and that decisions about it are informed.

The following example outlines how a feasibility study report would be set out.

Outline headings for a feasibility study report

Section	Key points
Introduction to the report	The terms of reference for the study (i.e. a list of rigorous, ordered instructions that clearly outline the issues that should be addressed in the study). Who carried out the study. Methodology and who was consulted in the production of the report.
Background to the report	Why was the report commissioned? What are the internal and external factors that prompted the parties to consider collaboration?
Profile of the parties	A brief and factual overview of the parties: their aims, structure, organisation and areas of operation.
Current levels of collaboration	A review of how the parties currently work together, for example liaison, referrals and joint initiatives. What has been the experience so far?
Strategic context	How might changes in policy, funding and commissioning priorities, user needs and ways of working drive the need for the organisations to merge? What might drive collaboration?
Potential for collaboration	What are the areas whereby merging could create some value?
Possible structures	What possible models are worth considering? Horizontal, vertical or group structure?
Potential gains	What might the potential benefits of merging be in terms of: • potential user gain; • savings and economies; • an ability to work at a bigger level; • future security?
Potential risks	What might be potential risks and losses as a result of merging in terms of: • services – responsiveness; • extra costs; • loss of identity and goodwill?
Issues that need addressing	An outline of the process of moving the issue forward. What would the process look like? Are there any significant issues or potential barriers that would need managing?
Conclusions	An overall summary.
Next steps	A suggested outline of the decisions that the parties need to make to move the issue forward (or not).

Example of an 'intent to merge' resolution

The Board of Directors of organisation A agrees to the following Memorandum of Understanding (MOU) between Organisation A and Organisation B:

1. *Each organisation will explore and propose negotiated terms of merger in good faith.*
2. *Each organisation may inform its constituents that this exploration is under way.*
3. *Neither organisation will pursue a merger with any other organisation during this exploration and negotiation period through X February 20XX.*
4. *Both organisations will cooperate in raising funds to support the costs associated with this process.*
5. *We authorise the individuals below to represent our organisation in exploring the advantages, risks and feasibility of a merger with Organisation B, and if appropriate, to negotiate a draft set of terms for such a merger.*

The merger team for our organisation will be:

- *JK, Chair, Board of Directors*
- *SL, Acting Executive Director*
- *TA, Board member*
- *JM, Board member*

We will receive a report from this team at each board meeting.

Adapted from Vergara-Lobo, Masaoka and Smith 2005

Communicating the merger

The talk of mergers will often create feelings of anxiety and stress within an organisation. A critical factor in determining the success of a merger process is the effectiveness of communication and how much those who are likely to be affected by the merger are involved. Managers need to develop a communication plan that has five component parts:

1. Clarity about why you are considering it

Do not assume that people have had the time or the opportunity to understand what might be driving the merger. Managers and trustees might need to spend time explaining the context and how the landscape on which the organisation operates is changing. By understanding the context and the bigger picture, people might be more able to appreciate why such a significant change is being considered.

2. A positive view

Managers and trustees need to create and develop a positive view of what a merged organisation might be able to do that cannot be done by staying apart. A useful way of doing this is by outlining what a successful vision of an effective merged organisation might look like.

3. Communication not broadcasting

Managers often approach communication as a one-way process. They convene a meeting to tell people what is happening. They over-rely on written communication. Lots of messages get sent, but few are received. The intention should be to create a dialogue in which people can ask questions, be listened to and, it is hoped, move to a position where they are actively involved in shaping the merger process. Managers must listen as much as they talk and create the space for full and proper discussions.

4. Explain the process

People need to understand the merger process. What is the timescale? When and how will key decisions be made? The process must be designed and steered in such a way that people are able to contribute to it, but also in a way that it does not drag on. Managers need to outline the process and mechanisms for influencing the process.

5. Encourage involvement and feedback

Throughout the merger process, the people affected by it need to be able to ask questions, express concerns and influence the process. If people are genuinely involved, there is more of a chance of their buying into the process or, at the very least, accepting it. Organisations need effective policies and procedures that can deal with staff concerns and grievances fairly and quickly during a major change process like a merger.

Governance

How a merged organisation is to be governed is obviously a question of huge importance and is certainly one that provides considerable anxiety. Whether it is a matter of one organisation transferring into another or a new organisation being formed, there is a need to be open to the partner organisation's needs and concerns. If handled sensitively, a merger can be a great opportunity to renew and develop the trustee board, bringing in new skills and building on the experience of more longstanding trustees.

One strategy is to invite all current trustees to continue as trustees in the new organisation. This is not always possible, as the new board might become too big and unwieldy. Sometimes there is a reduction in numbers, as some trustees see this as the opportunity to resign and move on to something new. In some organisations there is an agreement to recruit a new trustee specifically to chair the new organisation. This can be very helpful both internally (in alleviating anxieties about a takeover) and externally in being able to show that the merged organisation is a new venture and not just an amalgamation. However, the crucial factor is to ensure that the new board has the requisite skills, knowledge and experience to lead and govern the new organisation and fulfil its legal obligations. The governance arrangements must comply with the constitution of the merged organisation.

What is due diligence?

Due diligence is the process by which each organisation undertakes to satisfy themselves that a merger is in their best interests and will not leave the charity open to undue risk. It is a way of finding out more about the organisation with which you are merging. The nature and extent of the due diligence exercise varies, depending on the size and complexity of the organisations involved. The sorts of checks carried out should be proportionate to the size and nature of the proposal, the amount of income and expenditure involved, and the types of existing and planned activities.

A helpline staffed primarily by volunteers merging with an advice and information shop with a combined income of £90,000 will require a different level of due diligence from two charities with a combined income of £1.5 million per annum offering day-care services to adults with complex needs and employing specialist staff. However, the underlying aim is the same: to identify the potential risks of a merger and ensure that those risks are managed.

> *A due diligence exercise should provide sufficient information to enable potential merging charities to assess whether the merger is feasible and, if the merger proceeds, to identify and allocate most liabilities. In practice, charities may not be able to find some relevant documents, for example, contracts of employment or leases, and information will have to be obtained from trustees and employees. Part of the due diligence process for many charities will be assessing how much time and effort they want to put into pursuing enquiries about the other merging charities when seen against the likelihood of the risk of potential future liabilities.*
>
> Warburton 2001

In any due diligence process, both sets of trustees must undertake due diligence on behalf of their own organisation and they are responsible for deciding on the appropriate level of due diligence required. Some organisations carry out due diligence themselves. However, in larger or more complicated mergers, the trustees may want to pay professionals, usually accountants or solicitors, to help with the process. There are many examples of due diligence exercises but there are a number of broad headings that most checks fall under:

- Background and strategic issues
- Current and future financial situation including service delivery contracts
- Assets and liabilities
- Management and staff
- Legal issues

There are lots of issues that could be looked at during the due diligence process; deciding whether or not to include an issue in the due diligence process depends on how important it is to the merged organisation. If the service is dependent on IT to deliver a service directly to the public, such as through a telephone call centre, then it would seem prudent to ensure that IT systems are compatible prior to the merger or know how much time, money and staff training will be involved in making them compatible. However, if IT is used simply to administer the organisation then the compatibility of IT at the due diligence stage may be less important.

The following list is an example of the information two fairly similar medium-sized organisations shared in order to complete their due diligence process.

- Governing documents
- Lists of trustees
- Latest versions of business plans
- Most recent audited accounts
- Most recent finance reports, budget and cash flow
- Lists of significant assets
- Details of occupied premises and copies of leases
- Lists of insurances
- Statements regarding current and anticipated debt

- Statements regarding legal cases pending, anticipated or threatened
- Details of staff pension schemes and details of any liabilities arising from the scheme
- Lists of funders and projects being funded and for how long
- Lists of public service contracts, with amounts, restrictions and expiry dates
- Details of all employees: job titles, length of service, pay, pension contributions and employee benefits
- Contracts of employment and personnel policies
- Details of trade union representation where appropriate
- Details of ongoing disciplinary cases including Employment Tribunals
- Details of any premises including tenure (leasehold or freehold)
- Covenants or conditions which could affect the proposed merger (for example, the transfer of a lease will usually require the landlord's consent)

Before exchanging due diligence information, it is recommended that merging organisations should sign a confidentiality agreement. An example of a confidentiality agreement can be found in *Due Diligence Demystified: What It Is and How You Manage It* (see 'Further reading' on page 140).

When exchanging employee information, organisations need to ensure that the way this is done complies with the Data Protection Act. Whilst employee information required by TUPE can be exchanged (see page 120), employee information exchanged as part of due diligence that is wider than the TUPE requirements cannot be disclosed without either the consent of the individual or by anonymising the data.

The Charity Commission has a comprehensive checklist which is intended to be of use to trustees in understanding the due diligence process. It can be found on the Charity Commission website and as an appendix to its publication *Making Mergers Work: helping you succeed* (Charity Commission 2009). It includes what to do for each area and also indicates how to use the information, which questions to ask and when to seek expert help. It is broken down into three areas: commercial, financial and legal.

Complex mergers would need to assess all the areas in detail and this is where it is important to ensure that the exercise is proportionate to the size and nature of the proposal. Depending on the activities of the organisations merging, it may be necessary as part of the due diligence process to refer to other public bodies such as:

- the Criminal Records Bureau in cases when you are taking on staff or volunteers who require checks;
- the Land Registry where property or land is being transferred;
- HM Revenue and Customs when the new organisation will affect the charity's tax or trading arrangements, for example the merger takes the organisation over the threshold for VAT.

A due diligence exercise

Purpose

- To identify any key risks or ongoing liabilities.
- To identify any factors that trustees need to be aware of in considering a merger.
- To identify any issues that might block the merger process.

Factor	Potential risk or issue	Information source
Financial position	Financial standing of the organisation. Current financial position. Relationships between restricted and unrestricted funds. Ongoing financial commitments such as loan repayments and mortgages. Leases and commercial arrangements. Financial control system.	Past accounts. Current management accounts. Credit rating check. Contracts. Auditors' correspondence.
Governance	Ability to merge. Pension liabilities. Any requirements in the organisation's governing documents as to how a merger process must be carried out. Relationship to any subsidiary body. Compliance with governing document.	Governing document. Past annual reports. Correspondence with any regulatory bodies.
Employment issues	TUPE commitments. Ongoing staffing issues. Personnel processes.	Staff terms and conditions of employment. Staff handbook.
Management issues	Organisational performance. Internal problems.	Past and current business plan. Management committee and management team minutes.
Service issues	Contracts with commissioners. Future funding position. Funding agreements. Contract performance. Service quality. Operating standards.	Current contacts, service-level agreements. Performance measurement reports. Correspondence with funders and commissioners. Service evaluations. User complaints. Organisational manual. Health and safety policy and reports. Quality assurance awards Inspection or regulatory reports.

Designing the new merged organisation

At some point in a merger process, questions start being asked as to what the new merged organisation will look like and how it will operate. This involves constitutional issues as well as issues of internal structure.

If two charities are forming a completely new charity, a governing document will need to be prepared for the new charity and in most cases the new organisation will need to be registered as a charity well before the final merger date (otherwise the trustees and members of the former organisations would potentially be transferring charitable assets to a non-charitable organisation).

If one charity is dissolving into an existing charity, the merged organisation will be subject to the governing document of the existing charity. In some cases, constitutional changes may be needed to extend the charity's aims and objects, and these will need to be approved and registered before the merger takes place.

In terms of the internal structure, staff and volunteers are understandably keen to know where they will fit into the new structure. Service users, funders and other partners may also want to know how the new organisation will operate and be organised.

Staff structures and the way voluntary organisations are organised are often not deliberately designed. They are more a product of ad hoc planning and opportunity. Funding creates projects. Bits get added on. The organisation is overly influenced by the interests and preferences of individuals who work in it. Creating a newly merged organisation is an opportunity to think afresh and develop a robust and sustainable organisation. In designing a merged organisation, the following issues need to be avoided:

Overly detailed design

There is a tendency in pre-merger negotiations to try to ensure that each and every detail of how the merged organisation will operate is in place. Trying to do this will delay the merger process. A better course may be to agree overall structures and roles and leave detailed consideration to staff and managers to work on in the post-merger implementation stage. However, it is important to realise that individual staff will want to know as soon as possible how they will fit into the merged organisation (especially if there may be redundancies). With this in mind, try to avoid a long period of uncertainty or it can lead to resentment, anxiety, and poor morale (which is very hard to recover).

Simply aggregating what you already have

Simply slotting two organisations together is unlikely to deliver much value. The merger should be an opportunity to think about the most effective ways of organising and delivering services. If people carry on as before, it is hard to see the point in merging. A better starting point is to see the merger as a rare chance to design a new organisation that is modern, relevant and builds on the best elements of what went before.

Designing around individuals

In organisational change projects it is important to keep to a discipline of working out what you want to do and the best way to organise it, and then identifying the most effective way your staff can fit into the roles that are needed.

It is crucial to identify the roles and skills you need and then look at the ability of the current staff team to play them. A common error is to design organisations around the styles, preferences and skills of the people you already have in post. This limits the potential for development and can hold an organisation back. If staff are to move into new roles, the merger process will need fair and effective processes and procedures for supporting and helping them to do so.

The managers driving the merger need to build an atmosphere that encourages people to see the merger as a real opportunity to design and build an organisation that is relevant, modern and able to adapt to change. A good starting point is to try and identify what existing practices and structures work well and see how they can be replicated in the new organisation.

Organisations can be designed around a number of things:

- User needs: the issues and needs that service users commonly have.
- Geography: physical locations and boundaries.
- Service: the type of service that you are trained to provide, such as advice work or youth work.
- Income and funding streams: where the money to pay for the service comes from.

In designing new organisations, the following six points are worth considering:

1. What practices do you want to keep?

What works in the current structures? What do you want to do more of?

2. How can you improve the user experience?

Try to see the organisation outside–in: what must it be like to be a service user? How can you improve the service user's journey and experience of accessing, contacting and using the service?

3. How can technology improve your services?

Does technology give you an opportunity to communicate differently, involve people and open more accessible ways of using your services?

4. What choices can you offer?

One size rarely fits all. Can you offer different ways in to a service and a level of flexibility?

5. What support and management do you need?

How can the organisation's back office functions, such as administration, finance and supervision, best support the service delivery process?

6. What skills do you need?

What kinds of skills and expertise will staff need throughout the organisation? What kinds of competencies do you want to encourage in the new organisation?

Traditional organisational design models

Some traditional organisational design models include:

- **Functional design:** staff are organised within traditional occupational or professional boundaries. People doing the same type of job (such as housing management, fundraising or marketing) are clustered together in occupational groups.
- **Product or output-based design:** staff are grouped together to deliver a particular service, project, product or contract. They operate as a distinct unit within the organisation overall.
- **Matrix design:** staff with different skills and expertise are brought together to deliver a particular initiative or job. This design model is often very task-focused or temporary.

The Transfer of Undertakings (Protection of Employment) Regulations 2006 (TUPE)

TUPE will almost certainly apply to any mergers which involve paid staff. It is a complex area where legal advice should be sought at an early stage to ensure that it is done correctly and legal risks and obligations to staff are properly understood.

The principal purpose of TUPE legislation is to protect employees in instances where there is a service provision change or a change in the legal identity of the employer through transfer of an undertaking, or part of an undertaking, from one entity to another. The regulations govern the position of staff transferred from one organisation to another, protecting their terms and conditions and preserving continuity of employment. This means a merger cannot be used to downgrade salaries, holidays or other terms of employment unless employees specifically agree.

Organisations will need to provide full details of the employees being transferred, contracts of employment and working practices which may, in effect, have become contract terms. Because there is a legal duty to provide this information, the Data Protection Act allows this disclosure. However, care needs to be taken that it complies with data protection principles (for example. the information is secure, accurate and up to date) and is only used for the purposes of TUPE. There is also a duty to consult those who may be affected by the transfer; failure to do so in the ways laid out will result in penalties for the employers. It is important to note that the duty to consult is with employees in both the transferring organisation (the transferor) and the organisation to which it is being transferred (the transferee).

When people are not offered a post in the new structure a lot of work may need to be done. For example, when two people compete for the same job, if the unsuccessful person is to be made redundant, the terms of any redundancy deal should be clear from the outset to avoid disputes and recriminations. Even where this has been done, great care is needed to ensure such action does not amount to a breach of TUPE, and advice from employment law specialists will usually be needed.

TUPE protection continues after merger. This does not mean that organisations cannot therefore restructure or reduce the size of the workforce. However, it must show that the reason for doing so is an ETO (economic, technical or organisational) reason. (For instance, one example of an 'organisational' reason is where one organisation operates at such a distance from the merged organisation that it is not feasible or practical to transfer staff.) If the organisation fails to demonstrate an ETO reason then it will be open to challenge. The same is true in varying terms and conditions: if the changes are not because of the transfer, but a reason connected to the transfer which is an ETO reason, then the changes would potentially be legal. The same is true of variations which are unconnected to the transfer. However, it is often very difficult to identify changes which are genuinely exempt from TUPE – specialist advice will be needed if this is being considered.

TUPE: information which must be provided by the transferor

- The identity and age of employees.
- A statement of particulars of employment (see Section 1 of the Employment Rights Act 1996, which can be found at www.legislation.gov.uk). This statement will include the name of the employer and employee, the date employment started, and the date at which the employee's continuous employment started, including with previous employers. The statement also includes, among other things, the scale or rate of remuneration, intervals of payment, hours of work, holidays, incapacity benefit and pension entitlement, notice period, job title and place of work.
- Information on any disciplinary action taken against an employee or grievance raised by an employee in the past two years where the ACAS Code of Practice on Disciplinary and Grievance Procedure applies.
- Information on any court or tribunal case, claim or action brought by an employee against the transferor within the previous two years or that the transferor has reasonable grounds to believe that an employee may bring against the transferee arising out of the employee's employment with the transferor.
- Information on any collective agreement which will take effect after the transfer in its application in relation to the employee pursuant to Regulation 5(a) TUPE.
- Information relating to the use of agency workers:
  i. The number of agency workers working temporarily for and under the supervision and direction of the employer.
  ii. The parts of the employer's undertaking in which those agency workers are working.
  iii. The type of work those agency workers are carrying out.

Pensions

Occupational pensions were the one area where TUPE did not provide protection. However, the Transfer of Employment (Pension Protection) Regulations 2005 apply to transferring employee pensions and give more pension protection than that afforded by TUPE. Where a transferor (the organisation winding up) provides an occupational pension scheme, the transferee (the new organisation or the organisation being transferred into) will also have to provide a comparable scheme and must match employee contributions up to 6% into a stakeholder scheme.

Many charities in multi-employer defined benefit schemes (such as local authority schemes or group schemes) could be faced with great difficulties if, as a result of a merger, the organisation is deemed no longer to exist or its staff are under threat of redundancy. This can create a 'cessation liability', meaning that the charity must make up the deficit in the fund. It is important to take advice early in the merger process to establish if there could be an ongoing pensions liability and the likely extent of it.

At the time of writing, the government is carrying out a review of this issue, as it is recognised that pensions liability can be a major obstacle to mergers.

Register of Mergers

The Register of Charity Mergers was created by Parliament in the Charities Act 2006 (the provisions are now in the Charities Act 2011). It is administered by the Charity Commission. The purpose of this legislation was to:

> Ensure that, where charities have merged, any future legacies in their name will be applied to the successor charity directly, once the merger has been registered with the Commission. As such, future legacies should no longer require a scheme to apply the funds to the successor charity nor should it be necessary to leave shell charities on the Central Register of Charities to receive legacies.
>
> Charity Commission 2006

In general, when one charity merges into another charity and the original charity is dissolved, the Charity Commission should be asked to place the old charity on the Register of Mergers with details of the charity into which it has merged. Any subsequent gifts or legacies to the old charities then pass automatically to the merged charity, unless the will or documentation specifies otherwise.

However, it is not always that straightforward. The way in which the Act was drawn up was flawed, because wills often contain conditions such as 'if the charity no longer exists at the time of my death...' and technically a former charity would no longer exist if it had been wound up as part of a merger. So, charities are not always able to receive legacies left to them under their pre-merger names. As such, there are calls for an amendment to the Charities Act to address this issue and, in the meantime, many lawyers are advising merging charities to retain shell organisations post-merger to ensure that legacies are protected.

If charities have used a Vesting Declaration (a deed transferring title to property including land and buildings), then registration on the Register of Mergers is compulsory. If they have not used one, registration is voluntary, but if the former charity is to be wound up (not retained as a shell) it will almost always make sense to register the merger.

Restricted funds

Particular attention needs to be given in a merger process to handling funds that are restricted in special trusts or were designed to create a permanent endowment. (Permanent endowments are any assets of a charity, including land or investments, which the trustees are prohibited from spending because of a restriction in the charity's governing document.)

Such funds must be dealt with in accordance with the specific rules governing their use. It may be necessary to ensure that the funds are restricted or ring fenced within the new merged charity, or the terms might enable the funds to be transferred.

Note that changes in the Charities Act 2011 regarding permanent endowments mean that these restrictions are only an issue in rare cases. It is advisable in these cases to seek advice early on from charity law specialists or the Charity Commission to see how the funds can be transferred.

Maintaining a 'shell' organisation

In instances where there are legal barriers to asset transfer and the organisations holding the assets cannot be dissolved (such as with permanent endowments, legacy income or buildings that are subject to restrictive covenants preventing a sale), one solution is for the organisation to remain as a shell organisation but to function solely as a holding trustee for the organisation's assets. Further advice on this can be obtained from the Charity Commission or, where this is a significant issue, from professional advisors.

Post-merger integration

Once the organisation is legally merged, this is not the end of the story. Indeed one chief executive commented that this point was when the hard work really began! Post-merger integration is all about making the newly merged organisation work. It can cover the following issues:

- helping people to settle into new ways of working;
- ensuring that new structures and processes work;
- building a new identity and brand.

The work involved in designing a merger, negotiating the process and making it happen is so demanding that little time is spent on planning and managing what happens after the merger. Perhaps the biggest challenge is getting people to feel and behave as part of one organisation. This usually involves building a new organisational culture and helping people to contribute to it.

Case study: a merger in name only? The Westgrove Centre

Eighteen months after the formal merger took place, Westside Enterprise Centre and the Grove Community Outreach Project felt and operated in much the same ways that they had before the merger.

The idea to merge the two organisations had been suggested by the secretary of a local grants foundation who felt that both organisations could gain from working together as they had similar aims and worked in the same neighbourhoods.

The merger happened relatively quickly. A friendly solicitor drafted a new governing document and handled staff transfers to the new organisation. The new organisation was to be called 'The Westgrove Centre' as a neutral title. Staff job roles hardly changed at all, although the Manager of the Westside Enterprise Centre was asked to be the overall manager.

To ensure local relevance it was agreed that below the new management board there would be two steering groups to oversee the work of the Westside Centre and the Grove Project (see fig. 8.5).

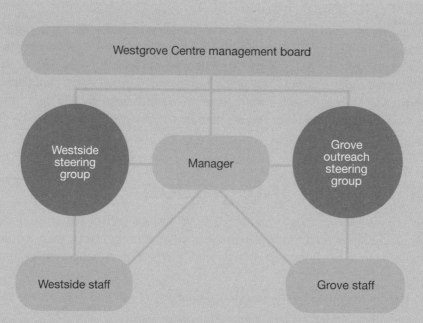

Fig. 8.5 Westside Centre and Grove Project steering groups

The two staff teams carried on as if little had changed. Indeed, although it clearly shouldn't have happened, the phone continued to be answered with the old name rather than with the new title. Very little joint working materialised. Staff and volunteers were reluctant to work together and wanted to stick with the working practices from the previous organisations. The steering groups started to operate as if they were in complete charge referring to the management board as a 'rubber stamping body'. The Manager felt that he was spending most of his time negotiating between the two parts. It was difficult to show any real gains that had come about from merging. In the next six months the new organisation would face some difficult decisions and challenges. He was not confident that it was strong enough to cope.

It was as if the organisation had merged on paper, but essentially stayed the same. On reflection, he commented:

> *During the merger process we concentrated too much on the technical issues such as sorting out the constitution, transferring staff and setting up a new structure. The real task was designing and building a new single organisation that built on the best bits of the previous organisations. During the merger process we spent too long reassuring staff that everything would be all right and that the merger was only a technical process. What we should have done is involve them in planning what sort of community project is needed locally and how a merged organisation could move into that role. The real work begins now!*

The following points can be useful in planning post-merger integration:

Don't write off the past

See the merger as a chance to combine what the previous parties did best. People may well be proud of what they helped to build, so the merger should be a continuation or an evolution of what was good. Sometimes managers are inclined to imply that the future is always a better place and that what has gone before had little value. This is liable to make people feel defensive.

Create opportunities for people to share and work together

During and after the merger process there need to be opportunities for staff to work together to identify and explore what they have in common and what skills and expertise are available to the newly merged organisation.

Have fair and open processes

The way in which people are slotted into the new structure needs to be transparent and fair and should not give any advantage to people from one party.

Go for a few quick and early wins

A few early successes, such as launching a new service or winning a contract, can help to create a feeling of momentum and progress as people start to see tangible gains and benefits from the merger. Share success.

Provide support

Staff may need practical support, training and help in adapting to new ways of working and developing new systems. Learning new things is the easy bit. The hard part is giving up what you have already been doing. Managers need to be available to provide coaching, support and practical help to aid the settling-in process.

Actively manage external relationships

Managers must plan how they will ensure that key relationships with supporters, partners and other external parties are maintained. After the merger launch, there needs to be an active process of maintaining relationships and communications and ensuring that the goodwill which might have existed towards the previous parties is transferred to the merged organisation.

Case study: five into one Cumbria CVS – a five-way merger

After much consideration, in March 2008 Cumbria CVS was established with the intention to provide a more efficient, stronger, more equitable and more accessible delivery of voluntary and community sector infrastructure support services across Cumbria and to maximise opportunities for funding.

The new organisation was the product of a complex merger between five well-established district councils for voluntary services based throughout Cumbria. The new organisation has been able to maintain local identity and local funding relationships, but has also been able to operate at a more strategic level and ensure that the sector is a key player at a county-wide level. It has also enabled the new organisation to develop specialist functions on a county basis that would not have been possible in five separate districts. Karen Bowen, Chief Officer of Cumbria CVS, said: 'On reflection, the merger was probably the best thing we ever did.'

The process of negotiating a merger of five organisations was, by its nature, a complicated one. Karen commented that some elements of the process such as due diligence and managing the human resource process were relatively straightforward compared with the more difficult task of building a new organisational identity and culture.

Four key learning points can be drawn from their experience:

1. **Coordinating the process is demanding.** Running a merger process will take up a lot of management time. There needs to be a clear project plan and a way of ensuring that staff and trustees in the participating organisations know what is going on.

2. **Building a new culture takes a long time.** It takes a while for people to 'feel part' of a new organisation.

3. **Managers need to actively support the transition process.** They can do practical things to encourage staff to feel part of one organisation. Cumbria CVS invested in staff awaydays, regular staff newsletters and encouraged managers to regularly work from local offices to help improve communication and work towards feeling part of one staff team.

4. **Things evolve.** Enacting the merger is a transitional process rather than a big event on a particular day. What was planned in the pre-merger process might be different from what is needed post-merger. Structures and systems evolve. Some flexibility, therefore, is needed.

Chapter nine
Making collaborative initiatives work

It is relatively easy to get out the drawing board and design elegant and imaginative structures for organisational collaboration. Indeed, in the voluntary sector there are some people who positively seem to enjoy drawing up organisational charts and amending constitutions! However, in our experience the real effort is in making a collaborative venture work, and this inevitably involves leading and managing the people who, as trustees, staff and volunteers, make up our organisations.

We would suggest that four issues need specific attention.

1. Managing expectations.
2. Coping with organisational culture.
3. Building new ways of working.
4. Encouraging teamwork and cooperation across organisational boundaries.

All of these require dedicated leadership and management. They also require a commitment to follow through decisions and ensure that progress is not blocked or delayed. The chair of a joint partnership board described her experience:

> It took ages to negotiate setting the partnership up. We had to work through three different drafts of a partnership agreement until we could come up with a structure and terms of reference that everyone could buy into. When we eventually got an agreement signed off by all the partners I was tempted to feel that it was all done. In reality, the work had just begun. The real work was getting trustees and staff to work together and overcome traditional boundaries. Collaboration is a big change project.

1. Managing expectations

In developing a collaborative venture, communication is a critical success factor. Communication should be about opening up a dialogue and managing people's expectations of what collaboration can bring.

A useful exercise is to identify which individuals and groups might have a stake in a collaborative venture. Once identified, you can then test out their concerns and perceptions of what collaborative working might bring and then see if you need to develop particular communication plans to engage with them. In a period of change, effective communication can be crucial in ensuring that people are usefully involved or, at the very least, do not block or frustrate the process because of misinformation or a misunderstanding of your motives.

The people who are leading the collaboration need to give thought to what message they send out. Our experience is that when the issue of organisations working together is first raised people often become very defensive or suspicious. Common perceptions are:

'Collaboration means merger.'

'X will take us over.'

'It is all about losing jobs.'

'It is the end for us.'

Such perceptions are often based on bitter experience. To overcome them, managers need to see communication as a two-way process in which people have an opportunity to influence and shape the outcome. A good starting point is to plan out the message that you want to get through. Consider the three elements in the following example:

Issue	Questions	Key message
Why are we considering this?	• What's driving this issue? • What's the context? • What do we want to achieve?	Although demand for our services remains high, generating income is getting harder. We want to find out if by linking up with similar organisations doing similar work we would have a stronger future. We want to see if it will help us to deliver better services for our clients.
What's our intention?	• What matters to us? • What's the purpose of this?	We would only consider working with people who share our core values and principles. It is about building on our success. We see this as a way of continuing and developing our work in partnership with others.
What's the process?	• What has been agreed so far? • What are the next steps? • How can people get involved?	So far the trustee board has only agreed to *consider* the option of collaboration and has asked the managers to develop some ideas as to with whom and how we could collaborate. After the managers have reported back, the board will agree how best to move it forward. Copies of all reports are available to all staff.

It is important to create a positive feeling about collaboration. The chief executive of a youth agency described how a key task for her was dealing with people's anxieties and creating a positive vision about what might be possible:

Finding reasons not to do it became a lot of people's default position. That masked a lot of concerns about job security and where they would fit in. We had to do a lot of work to make the case to people that collaboration was about making us stronger and that by being a stronger organisation it could open up more opportunities to develop services, increase our profile and thereby be a more sustainable organisation.

There is a danger that the method used to communicate can get in the way of good communication. All too often people overuse written materials such as email, which means that communication is predominantly one-way and offers little opportunity for feedback or contribution. Managers must be available and visible. They also need to find ways of enabling staff and others to be involved in the process and encourage staff to help shape the process. To do this, an atmosphere of transparency and openness should be encouraged.

2. Coping with the organisational culture

Organisational culture is what holds an organisation together. It is made up of the beliefs, traditions and assumptions that have been built up over time. Organisational culture is rarely ever written down or recorded, but it can influence everything an organisation does and how it does it. It creates organisational identity and style, and influences the relationships both inside and outside the organisation. Understanding culture can be complicated. It will have evolved over time and is constantly changing. In organisations of any size there might be a number of different cultures or subcultures operating. Organisational culture represents an unwritten rule book that determines how things get done.

This culture can be positive or negative, fixed or static, or even contradictory. A positive culture allows people to embrace new ideas and be open to change. A negative culture can mean that people are very defensive and see everything as a threat. If it is too strong it can be very difficult to bring about change or introduce new ideas.

Getting organisations with different cultures to work together can be fraught with difficulties. What seem like small issues can frequently become a major symbolic issue. For example, an attempt to develop a joint partnership between two agencies working around mental health ran into difficulties about what to call the people who used the service. Staff from one agency who were mainly from a self-help and campaigning background preferred to call people 'users' or 'members'. Staff from the other agency, who were mainly from a clinical or healthcare background, preferred to call them 'patients' or 'clients'. A failure to resolve such a basic issue stored up problems that were to crop up later.

⚙ Case study: culture clash

After much negotiation and discussion, two organisations involved in social care agreed to share some services and run two joint projects. This involved staff from both organisations working together, referring clients and in some cases jointly delivering services.

Three months in, the initiative hit a number of problems. Several minor issues developed into conflicts between the organisations. On several occasions mistakes were made and communication between organisations became poor. A level of frustration started to grow. Misunderstandings and poor communication between the two teams started to increase and affect the service that was being delivered to clients.

The management committee chairs and managers from both organisations agreed to meet with an independent consultant to explore the issues. As part of the exercise, both parties were asked to talk about the culture, beliefs and assumptions that dominated their respective organisations.

Their comments are summarised in the following table.

Organisation A	Cultural factor	Organisation B
'Everyone should be involved in all decisions.'	Organisational style	'We aim to be professional and businesslike.'
'It is important to make sure that trustees, staff and volunteers know what is going on. We need to take time to ensure that they are involved.'	Forward planning	'Things are changing fast. It is important that we can be strategic and focused. We have to be able to respond quickly to new initiatives.'
'Our service model has taken years to develop. We know it is what our users want and appreciate.'	Service delivery	'We are keen to learn new things and are always keen to find new ways of doing things.'
'We treat people like individuals – we personalise things.'	Service style	'Our services need to operate in a consistent way. Training, policies and procedures are in place to back this up.'
'Not much really changes – we should stick to what we do best.'	Strategy	'There are loads of possibilities and opportunities out there. Standing still isn't an option.'
'We try to manage by consensus. It is much better if people understand and support where we are going.'	Management style	'Managers are employed to give a lead.'
'This is a people business. It is important to keep bureaucracy to a minimum.'	Systems	'We need procedures and processes to do our job properly and meet funders' expectations.'
'It is important that staff are valued and treated with respect. This place is more than a job.'	Employment style	'We have sound and comprehensive human resource systems.'

It was significant that this was the first time that the issue of different working styles and cultures had been properly discussed between the two organisations. In putting together the joint venture, all the attention had been on the structure and the content of the formal agreement. They had focused on the technicalities and not on how to make it work.

The managers recognised that they had a major issue to tackle. Both organisations were committed to the joint venture. Both of them were also committed to working together in the interests of their users. However, differences of approach were threatening their ability to deliver.

Over the next six weeks the managers agreed the following steps which were designed to encourage an exchange of information and learning between the organisations:

● Regular joint staff events: training, team building and social activities designed to highlight what united both staff teams.

● A programme of staff visits and short-term secondments to encourage staff to learn about each other's organisation.

● Setting up a task group to design a common website for new users.

The managers also agreed a simple procedure where any problem connected to how the organisations worked would be quickly referred to the managers who would then try to resolve it as quickly as possible. The managers agreed to focus on finding a solution and not on discussing which way of working was right.

The joint venture seems to have survived the cultural storm. There appears to be a level of understanding and appreciation between the staff teams that the organisations have different histories and cultures, but are committed to getting the best for the service user.

One of the managers reflected on the process:

I never really understood how crucial it is to understand the importance of organisational culture. It's the glue that holds things together. To get the joint venture to work we had to invest time in learning about each other and in particular avoid competitive point-scoring arguments about whose way of doing things was best. It's been a long process, but tackling culture has been critical to success.

The following points can be useful in tackling culture in a collaborative venture:

Explore what the culture is

Before you try to change a culture, first work out what it is. Managers need to spend time working out what the beliefs, assumptions and traditions are which have created the prevailing culture. In a collaborative venture, managers should try to understand the history, key events and background that have moulded each partner. They must listen and observe how the organisation really works before trying to change it.

Decide what you want to be

The people leading the collaborative venture need to be clear about what kind of shared culture they want to create. They must be able to articulate a clear and simple view of how the organisation should work covering the following issues:

● **Ethos:** what are the core values that unite the parties to the collaboration? What do we all stand for?

● **Principles:** what are the key issues that hold us together?

● **Treatment:** how should the people who use the organisation expect to be treated? What should their status be?

Managers need to find ways of explaining and illustrating these issues in practical and accessible ways.

Focus on behaviours

It is useful to identify what people can do to support collaborative ventures. Identifying such behaviours can help to encourage collaboration and build a new and positive shared culture. Practical support needs to be given to allow staff to develop new skills and learn from others.

Don't write off the past

In a change project managers often make the critical mistake of implying that the past is entirely negative and that their proposed change is a much better option. A worker in a housing project described how a planned merger was introduced:

> *Senior managers seemed to imply that the organisation that we had worked hard to build up was no longer viable or needed and that the only option was to merge with a bigger organisation. They ignored the shared history, pride and sense of identity we had built up. No wonder we reacted negatively!*

Build on what works

A successful collaborative initiative is one which has effectively shared what works. A useful process to go through at the start, therefore, is to look at how successful or effective practices can be replicated across a collaborative venture. A successful organisational change project is likely to be evolutionary in that it builds on what works well.

3. Building new ways of working

Once formally established, a collaborative venture will usually test the traditional ways in which people have worked and been managed. Some of the key changes might include:

- staff having to work in new teams and with new managers;
- having to manage services or organisational functions across a number of sites or locations;
- the need for systems to coordinate activities, communicate on a bigger scale and create a seamless journey for service users.

It is worthwhile to ensure that there are practical and legally watertight processes in place to support and encourage staff to work in new ways, such as:

- clear and effective personnel procedures for negotiating changes in an employee's job role;
- sound and efficient systems for internal communication;
- processes and procedures for staff to raise concerns and grievances and provide feedback;
- processes to manage people and functions across different locations;
- training and support activities to help people work together and learn from each other.

At the start of the process it is important to check that all staffing procedures are in place and are clear and legally up to date. The worst time to draw up a procedure is when you need it!

In creating any new venture it is important to ensure that its overall chance of success is not reduced by minor sticking points. Relatively small issues such as the inability to get computer systems to work together or a lack of common protocols or people working in different ways can easily frustrate collaborative ventures. Managers need to be able to act fast to solve problems that might get in the way of effective joint working.

Choosing to work with another organisation will usually involve having to make compromises and possibly giving up some things. It can involve a loss of some organisational autonomy and independence which is counterbalanced by the belief that by joining forces there will be a greater gain. The director of a training agency described how working in an alliance with other providers has changed how he now operates:

> In the past I had a pretty free rein to do what I thought was best. Now, I feel obliged to take my alliance partners into account. So, for example, if a new funding opportunity emerges or I see an opportunity for expanding into a new business area, I now feel that I should check it out with my alliance partners to see if we should work together or to make sure that I am not stepping on anyone's toes, whereas in the past I could do what I thought best. Equally, I would expect my alliance partners to consult me. This has slowed things down, but I hope it will pay off in the longer term.

⚙ Case study: the debugging group

Two months into the merger that led to the creation of the West End Cares Trust most people agreed it had been the right thing to do. However, a range of smaller issues were taking up a lot of staff and management time. The Trust was the product of the merger of two long-established social care agencies each with its own traditions, policies, procedures and practices. The management team of the new organisation had approved an operations manual which set out a single set of policies and procedures. Useful as this was, it did not cover all situations.

What seemed like quite minor issues, such as how to handle a situation or which working practice to follow, would often suddenly become a big issue and create tensions and conflicts between staff. Usually, discussions about what to do ended up in an argument about which of the previous organisations had the best policies and practices.

The Director of the Trust decided that the way forward would be to put together a small group of staff who became known as 'the debugging group' to resolve post-merger problems. The membership of the group was carefully selected to include a representative number of staff from the two previous organisations and a newly appointed manager who could bring a fresh perspective.

In its six months of operation, the debugging group dealt with a range of issues from casework recording systems, problems with email and procedures for approving staff training requests. In its time, the group developed a useful problem-solving approach. One of its members described how it developed:

> Both of the organisations had had very established ways of doing things. Pretty soon we realised that it would not work if all we did was arbitrate about which was the best one. We worked hard to focus on developing the best way of doing something and avoiding turning everything into a competition or argument about who had the best approach. It was often easier to suggest a new way built on the best aspects that existed in both organisations. Sometimes we had to get people together to focus on the bigger picture rather than a debate about who did it best.

After six months the group closed. Its work was seen as having been successful in helping to build a new and united way of working across the Trust.

4. Encouraging teamwork and cooperation across organisational boundaries

For collaboration to work, a culture of teamwork and cooperation needs to be built across traditional boundaries. This can be a slow and difficult process as it means getting staff and trustees to feel part of a bigger venture and to see the bigger picture. This is often difficult because people focus in on their project and resist engaging on a wider scale. The coordinator of a community enterprise consortium outlined her experience of this:

> We deliver what should be the same service across three different projects at three locations. Inevitably, there will be peaks and troughs in how busy people are. On occasions, we have tried to shift resources from one place to another to cope with demand on a temporary basis. Project leaders have done their utmost to block this. They see moving resources around as all about losing their 'empire'. They would prefer to see things not being used rather than be loaned to someone else.

A useful approach is to commit to a win-win approach rather than a win-lose style of managing and operating:

Win-win	Win-lose
● I'll focus on the bigger picture.	● I'll look after my bit.
● Let's find the best way of doing it.	● I'll do it my way.
● I'll give to get.	● I'll wait until someone else gives.
● Let's find a way of solving the problem.	● Let's talk about whose fault it is.

Moving to a win-win approach often requires a different way of operating. Managers need to take personal responsibility for encouraging and supporting behaviour that encourages effective collaborative working. The following tools and techniques have been used in different organisations to break down boundaries and encourage joint working:

- **Joint training:** bringing staff teams together to learn together or to share practice.
- **Team building:** events and activities, usually held on an offsite location, to help people get to know each other and open up positive communication.
- **Secondments:** moving staff into different roles on a temporary basis.
- **Task groups:** creating a representative team to work together for a limited duration to complete a predetermined task.
- **Benchmarking:** getting groups of staff to look outside the organisation to identify best practice in similar organisations and compare their approach.
- **Shadowing:** staff observing each other to see how they work.
- **Early wins:** focusing efforts on solving a couple of obvious problems early on in the life of a collaborative venture.

Evaluating collaboration

It is worthwhile to set time aside to evaluate how a collaborative initiative is working. Doing an evaluation in the life of a joint venture can deliver many benefits, including:

- identifying if the collaborative venture is living up to its expectations;
- identifying problems in how it is working that need tackling;
- producing evidence to use with funders and commissioners;
- acknowledging progress and recognising how far people have progressed;
- identifying issues and opportunities to build into future strategies.

There are two types of evaluation: programme evaluation, which focuses on what the collaborative venture has been able to deliver, and process evaluation, which looks at how the initiative is working and is being managed:

Programme evaluation questions

- What have we been able to achieve as a result of collaborating?
- What difference has working together made for our users and communities?
- Did we achieve our original plan?
- What else have we achieved?
- What feedback have we had from users?

Process evaluation questions

- How is the collaborative initiative working?
- Is it organised effectively?
- How is the collaboration governed?
- Are all partners engaged and involved?
- How might we improve how we work?

For evaluation to be effective, it needs to have time set aside for it. It should be an opportunity to reflect and take stock on progress to date. Some time and resources might have to be built into budgets to pay for the cost of surveying people, collecting data and possibly even employing external evaluators to organise the process and bring an external and independent perspective.

It is important that all parties are willing to be open in the evaluation and see it as a process to make what they have stronger and more effective.

Example: evaluating collaboration

Name of collaborative venture: Highway Debt Project: a three-year joint venture to run a money-management awareness programme.

Parties to it: Highway Advice Centre (lead body)
Highway Neighbourhood Project
Highway Church

What has the collaboration achieved so far?

Tangible achievements	Intangible achievements
• A successful schools project was delivered involving more than 400 students. • Three debt-awareness training courses were run for the housing dept. • 'Your money' pack was designed and published. 600 packs were distributed. • Local media coverage was attracted, including a two-page feature. • An inter-agency steering group was established. • 145 active cases were referred to us by other advice agencies and other organisations	• Very good relations were established with key agencies. • Greater public awareness about debt. • The local council was very supportive of our work. • Local advice agencies are now more skilled in dealing with debt and money issues.

As a result of collaborating what are we able to do now that we could not have done in the past?
• Having a dedicated campaign about debt.
• Being able to start to influence local policy makers.

How does the collaboration work?
• *What levels of participation and engagement do we have?* Usually good – steering group meetings are well attended by the three partners.
• *Is the work fairly allocated?* There is some concern that the Advice Centre as lead body has all the responsibility and is required to do all of the administration and reporting.
• *Are risks fairly apportioned?* Yes.
• *Are there any particular issues or sticking points that have made collaboration difficult?* We need to establish a common client referral process: issues of confidentiality and technology need to be worked on.

Future perspectives
• *Do we have any longer-term ideas about future collaborative working?* Should we package the schools training programme and try to sell it to other areas?
• *What are our short- to medium-term plans?*
  – We need to organise a mid-point review with our funder.
  – There is a possibility of another agency wanting to join the partnership.
• *Are there any action points as a result of this evaluation?*
  – Review the lead-body role and workload.
  – Set up task group to establish a common client referral process.

Exercise: evaluating collaboration

Name of collaborative venture:

Parties to it:

What has the collaboration achieved so far?

Tangible achievements	Intangible achievements

As a result of collaborating what are we able to do now that we could not have done in the past?

How does the collaboration work?

- *What levels of participation and engagement do we have?*

- *Is the work fairly allocated?*

- *Are risks fairly apportioned?*

- *Are there any particular issues or sticking points that have made collaboration difficult?*

Future perspectives
- *Do we have any longer-term ideas about future collaborative working?*

- *What are our short- to medium-term plans?*

- *Are there any action points as a result of this evaluation?*

References

Ainsworth, David (2012), 'Work Programme subcontractor to cease trading due to lack of working capital', www.thirdsector.co.uk, 16 July

The Audit Commission (1998), *A Fruitful Partnership: Effective Partnership Working*, London, Audit Commission Publications

Plummer, John (2009), 'RNIB backs new charity collaboration model', *Third Sector*, 30 June

Cairns, Ben, Margaret Harris and Romayne Hutchison (2003), *Key Findings on Voluntary Sector Mergers*, Centre for Voluntary Action Research

Charity Commission (2003), *RS4 Collaborative Working and Mergers*, Liverpool, Charity Commission, Crown Copyright

Charity Commission (2006), *Operational Guidance: Register of Charity Mergers: Sections 75C, D, E and F of the Charities Act 1993*, Liverpool, Charity Commission

Charity Commission (2009), *Making Mergers Work: Helping You Succeed*, Liverpool, Charity Commission, Crown Copyright

Sayer Vincent (2008), *Mergers Made Simple*, www.sayervincent.co.uk, CFDG

Social Finance (2009), *Charity Mergers: Tackling the Issues in Practice*, London, Social Finance Ltd

Warburton, Jean (2001), *Mergers – A Legal Good Practice Guide*, University of Liverpool Charity Law Unit

Vergara-Lobo, Alfredo, Jan Masaoka and Sabrina L. Smith (2005), *The M Word: A Board Members Guide to Mergers*, San Francisco, CompassPoint Nonprofit Services

Further reading

Publications which have websites cited can be found free of charge on those websites.

Charity Commission (2010), *Choosing to Collaborate: Helping You Succeed*, www.charitycommission.gov.uk, Crown copyright

Charity Commission (2009), *Collaborative Working and Mergers* (CC34), www.charitycommission.gov.uk, Crown copyright

Collaborative Working Unit (2006), *Merger: A Model of Collaborative Working*, London, NCVO

Morgan, Gareth G. (2013), *Charitable Incorporated Organisations*, London, Directory of Social Change

NCVO (2006), *Due Diligence Demystified: What It Is and How You Manage It*, London, NCVO

Office of Fair Trading (2009), *Quick Guide to Competition Law: Compliance Protecting Businesses and Consumers from Anti-Competitive Behaviour* (OFT1330), www.oft.gov.uk, Crown copyright

Office of Fair Trading (2011), *How Your Business Can Achieve Compliance with Competition Law* (OFT1341), www.oft.gov.uk, Crown copyright

Office of Fair Trading (2011), *Company Directors and Competition Law* (OFT1340), www.oft.gov.uk, Crown copyright

Sayer Vincent (2011), *Collaborative Working Made Simple*, www.sayervincent.co.uk, Sayer Vincent

Williams, Ian (2007), *Charity Talks: When to Collaborate and When to Compete?*, London, Cass Business School, Centre for Charity Effectiveness

Index

What else can DSC do for you?

Let us help you to be the best you possibly can be. DSC equips individuals and organisations with expert skills and information to help them provide better services and outcomes for their beneficiaries. With the latest techniques, best practice and funding resources all brought to you by our team of experts, you will not only boost your income but also exceed your expectations.

Publications

With over 100 titles we produce fundraising directories and research reports, as well as accessible 'how to' guides and best practice handbooks, all to help you help others.

Training

The voluntary sector's best-selling training – 80 courses covering every type of voluntary sector training.

In-house Training

All DSC courses are available on your premises, delivered by expert trainers and facilitators. We also offer coaching, consultancy, mentoring and support.

Conferences and Fairs

DSC conferences are a fantastic way to network with voluntary sector professionals whilst taking part in intensive, practical training workshops.

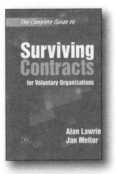  

Funding Websites

*DSC's funding websites provide access to thousands of trusts, grants, statutory funds and corporate donations. You won't get more funders, commentary and analysis anywhere else. Demo our sites **free** today.*

Trust**funding**.org.uk

Government**funding**.org.uk

Company**giving**.org.uk

Grantsfor**individuals**.org.uk

Visit our website today and see what we can do for you:

www.**dsc.org.uk**

Or contact us directly: publications@dsc.org.uk

@DSC_Charity
For top tips and special offers